W9-BVT-072

To buy books in quantity for corporate use
or incentives, call **(800) 962–0973**
or e-mail **premiums@GlobePequot.com.**

Library of Congress Cataloging-in-Publication
Data is available on file.

ISBN: 978-0-7627-7059-5

Cover design by Simon Goggin

Printed and bound in China

10 9 8 7 6 5 4 3 2 1

# EXPLORING THE CITY OF ROME IN AD 300

# CONTENTS

## 1

## A CONCISE BACKGROUND

## 2

## THE CITY OF ROME

## 3

## SURROUNDING AREAS

## 4

### ENTERTAINMENT
### ON A BUDGET

## 6

### REFERENCES
### AND RESOURCES

## 5

### PRACTICAL
### CONSIDERATIONS

# INTRODUCTION: WHEN THIS BOOK WAS WRITTEN

THIS BOOK IS WRITTEN TO OFFER ADVICE FOR TRAVELERS TO ROME, THE GREATEST CITY ON EARTH, IN THE YEAR AD 300. TO PLACE THIS IN CONTEXT THE FOLLOWING IS A TIMELINE OF ROMAN HISTORY, WITH DATES EXPRESSED AS THE NUMBER OF YEARS BEFORE THE DATE OF WRITING.

## A HISTORICAL TIMELINE

| | |
|---|---|
| 1052 years ago | Foundation of Rome |
| 808 years ago | Foundation of the republic |
| 689 years ago | Gauls sack Rome |
| 611 years ago | Via Appia built |
| 563 years ago | First gladiatorial fights |
| 563–540 years ago | First Punic War with Carthage |
| 519 years ago | Via Flaminia built (Rome to Ariminum) |
| 518–501 years ago | Second Punic War |
| 467 years ago | Greece and Macedonia conquered |
| 448–445 years ago | Third Punic War ends, Carthage destroyed |
| 390–387 years ago | War with Italian allies (the Social War) |
| 348 years ago | Julius Caesar begins a civil war |
| 343 years ago | Assassination of Julius Caesar |
| 330 years ago | Octavian defeats Anthony and Cleopatra at Actium and conquers Egypt |
| 326 years ago | Octavian begins the rule of emperors |
| 306 years ago | Rome divided into 14 regions |
| 286 years ago | Death of Augustus (Octavian) |
| 257 years ago | Claudian Conquest of Britannia |
| 234 years ago | Revolt of the Jews begins |
| 231 years ago | Civil war; the year of the four emperors |
| 230 years ago | Capture of Jerusaleum |
| 220 years ago | Vesuvius erupts; Colosseum dedicated |

| | |
|---:|:---|
| 185–183 years ago | Jewish Revolt |
| 107 years ago | Civil war |
| 88 years ago | All freeborn subjects made citizens |
| 62 years ago | Revolt in Africa and Italy |
| 50–22 years ago | Invasions and revolts divide the provinces |
| 30 years ago | Rome's new walls built |
| 16 years ago | Accession of Diocletian |
| 15 years ago | Maximian becomes caesar |
| 14 years ago | Maximian made co-emperor |
| 12 years ago | Revolt of Carausius and loss of Britannia |
| 7 years ago | Galerius and Constantius Chlorus appointed as caesars |
| 4 years ago | Carausius defeated, Britannia recovered |
| 4–2 years ago | Maximian restores order in Gaul and Africa |
| 2 years ago | Persians acknowledge Roman power beyond the Tigris |

WHAT TO EXPECT

## MEASURING TIME

The Romans use several systems for the measurement of years. The chief method is to name the two consuls who held office during the year. This year is the second time both consuls Constantius and Galerius have held office jointly. Sometimes they use the reigning year of the current emperor—in this case, Diocletian. Occasionally they count back to the traditional year of the founding of Rome.

# INTRODUCTION: THE GREATEST EMPIRE ON EARTH

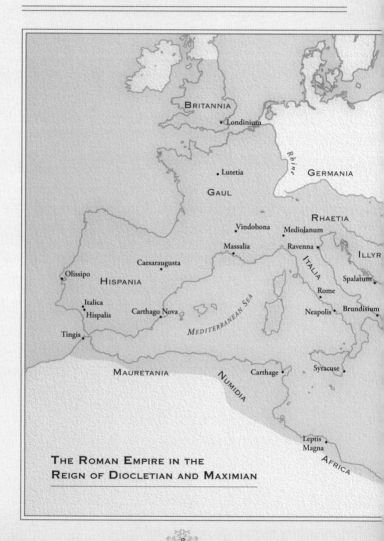

BRITANNIA

Londinium

Rhine

GERMANIA

Lutetia

GAUL

RHAETIA

Vindobona

Mediolanum

Massalia

Ravenna

ITALIA

ILLYR

Caesaraugusta

Olissipo

HISPANIA

Spalatum

Rome

Italica

Carthago Nova

Brundisium

Hispalis

MEDITERRANEAN SEA

Neapolis

Tingis

MAURETANIA

NUMIDIA

Carthage

Syracuse

Leptis
Magna

AFRICA

## THE ROMAN EMPIRE IN THE REIGN OF DIOCLETIAN AND MAXIMIAN

THE CITY OF ROME STANDS AT THE HEART OF THE GREATEST
EMPIRE ON EARTH. LARGER AND MORE DIVERSE THAN ANY
OTHER, ROME HAS MANY DIFFERENT FACES, REFLECTING THE
DIVERSITY OF THE EMPIRE'S INHABITANTS.

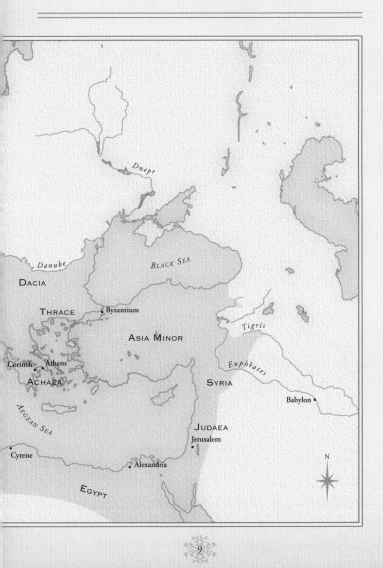

# INTRODUCTION: MAKING THE MOST OF YOUR TRIP

SINCE ROME IS A CITY FAR LARGER THAN ANY THAT YOU MAY HAVE VISITED BEFORE (EVEN ALEXANDRIA, IN EGYPT, IS THREE TIMES SMALLER), YOU WILL NEED TO PLAN YOUR VISIT CAREFULLY SO YOU DON'T WANDER BEWILDERED AMONG THE URBAN CROWDS GOING ABOUT THEIR BUSINESS.

Once you have established a place of residence in the city, you would be well advised to make yourself known to one of the *vicus'* (neighborhoods') two *vicomagistri* (administrators). These can be found at the local shrine, often located at the largest crossroad. This is also the local information hub, where news and gossip are exchanged freely. The locals are used to visitors and the constant flow of migrants to the city, so your own appearance in the city should be pretty unremarkable to its residents.

Of course, a visitor to Rome should spend most of his or her time in the city, but some visits further afield should also be undertaken. Given the attractions in the city and the surrounding areas, it is suggested that travelers spend half their visit within the city itself, but allow a similar amount of time for visits to neighboring regions, as well as a trip to the Bay of Naples.

## THE CLIMATE

The climate in Rome is mostly pleasant, but visitors are advised to avoid August. Most Romans try to leave the city in this month; not only is it hot and unpleasant, but the risk of ill health seems to be greater in the summer months.

Winter in Rome can not only be cold but also extremely wet, and visitors are advised to equip themselves with suitable clothing. In the mountains—of which a number are visible from Rome itself—snow is frequent in winter.

When the melting snow in the spring combines with heavy rain, the Tiber frequently bursts its banks, flooding low-lying parts of the city. Therefore visitors in spring are advised to find lodgings on one of the seven hills rather than in the valleys between.

The pleasantness of the climate is not the only factor in choosing the time of your visit. Roman medical thought, on which the volume by Celsus, *De Medicina*, is

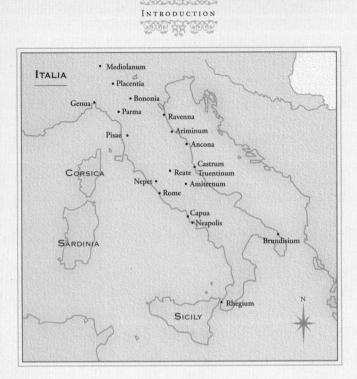

### ITALIA

- Mediolanum
- Placentia
- Bononia
- Genua
- Parma
- Ravenna
- Pisae
- Ariminum
- Ancona
- CORSICA
- Castrum Truentinum
- Reate
- Nepet
- Amiternum
- Rome
- SARDINIA
- Capua
- Neapolis
- Brundisium
- Rhegium
- SICILY

N

illuminating, suggests that spring and winter are the safest seasons for a person's health and that autumn, due to the changeability of the season, causes the greatest illness. Bearing in mind this medical advice, as well as the above observations on climate, visits are best made in the months of March, April, and May if possible.

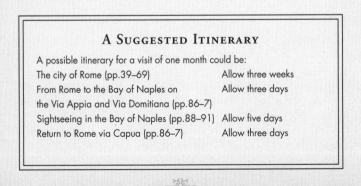

## A SUGGESTED ITINERARY

A possible itinerary for a visit of one month could be:

| | |
|---|---|
| The city of Rome (pp.39–69) | Allow three weeks |
| From Rome to the Bay of Naples on the Via Appia and Via Domitiana (pp.86–7) | Allow three days |
| Sightseeing in the Bay of Naples (pp.88–91) | Allow five days |
| Return to Rome via Capua (pp.86–7) | Allow three days |

# A CONCISE
# BACKGROUND

*Europe and Asia now stand united under Rome; all
are citizens and none can be described as foreigners.
Roads and sea-lanes link the peoples of the empire in
ways that are unprecedented, and Rome has surpassed
all the great civilizations of the past, improving upon
the achievements of the Greeks and achieving greater
mastery of her empire than ever the Persians or
Egyptians did. Few cities contain garrisons, but all are
loyal and flourish.*

*Who directs this vast empire? The emperors Diocletian
and Maximian, aided by two caesars. They have put
right the conflicts of the past century, and all agree that
Rome is now restored and her future secure.*

# HISTORY: FROM FOUNDATION TO REPUBLIC

SOME 1053 YEARS AGO ROMULUS, A DESCENDANT OF FUGITIVES FROM THE CITY OF TROY, FOUNDED THIS GREAT CITY. FOR 244 YEARS THE NEW CITY WAS RULED BY KINGS, TO BE FOLLOWED BY A REPUBLIC THAT LASTED FOR ALMOST 500 YEARS, UNTIL THE CURRENT SYSTEM OF EMPERORS WAS ESTABLISHED 327 YEARS AGO.

Romulus and a few followers founded Rome on the Palatine Hill. Their numbers grew as criminals and exiles from other cities in the region flocked to the city. There was a problem, though: there were no women, and the city looked as though it would last but a single generation. The Romans petitioned the Sabine cities in the region to have the right of marriage (*conubium*) with their daughters, but the Sabine fathers mocked such a proposal.

It was only through a ruse that Romulus ensured his city survived. He invited Rome's neighbors to attend a splendid set of games in the Circus Maximus, and insisted that the men and women should sit separately. Once the Sabines were seated, the Romans seized the women. Their fathers and brothers returned home for weapons and fought the Romans, but the war ceased when the Sabine women, now the wives of the Romans, pleaded with both their husbands and their fathers for peace.

## THE RULE OF KINGS

Romulus and his successor Numa brought many laws and customs into being. They were followed by a series of kings—good, bad, and indifferent—many of whom were from Etruria. Much of the city was laid out at this time, and you will still see elements of it today: the main drain or Cloaca Maxima, the ruins of the Servian walls, and it is also thought that the forum dates from this time.

Many things may have caused the end of the rule of the kings of Rome, but the most popular fable is that Tarquin the Proud was besotted with the beautiful but virtuous Lucretia. As was often the way with kings, he wouldn't take no for an answer and, consumed with desire for this married woman, he raped her. Lucretia revealed the incident to Lucius Junius

## REMUS

What about Romulus' brother Remus? Rome should have been founded by Remus on the Aventine Hill. After all, he won the competition to decide Rome's location—seeing more birds from there than his brother did from the Palatine—but Romulus lied that he saw the greater number.

Romulus was later to kill his brother—a sorry tale and, you might think, not one the Romans would be inclined to make up.

However, visitors will encounter more than seventy versions of the tale of Romulus and Remus. Does this mean the story is not true, and if so, then what purpose does Remus' fate serve in a fable? Is he simply a victim of his brother's cunning? These are subjects that all Romans have an opinion on, and visitors can easily hear some of the many different versions told in the bars, barber shops, and at the crossroads of the city.

*Cast out as infants, the brothers Romulus and Remus were suckled by a she-wolf and survived to found Rome.*

Brutus, among others, and then plunged a dagger into her own body. Brutus took the dagger and swore vengeance on her violator.

Her body was displayed in the forum, the citizens rallied to the cause, and Tarquin, the last king, was expelled.

# HISTORY: THE ROMAN REPUBLIC

THE NEW REPUBLIC GAVE POWER TO ROME'S ARISTOCRATS, BUT AT THE SAME TIME ENSURED THAT NO SINGLE MAN COULD WIELD THE POWER OF A KING, WITH TWO CONSULS BEING ELECTED EVERY YEAR. THESE MEN WERE ALSO, TO BEGIN WITH AT LEAST, THE COMMANDERS OF THE ARMY, SO WITH EACH NEW YEAR WOULD COME A NEW GENERAL TO WAGE WAR AGAINST ROME'S NEIGHBORS. GRADUALLY THE ENTIRE PENINSULA FELL UNDER ROMAN CONTROL, NEW LANDS WERE CONQUERED AND NEW COLONIES FOUNDED.

Rome's conquests brought her into conflict with the great trading city of Carthage, first in Sicily and then in Spain, each associated with a brutal struggle between these two great cities.

It once looked as though the whole of Italy might fall to the Carthaginians; but the resilience of the Roman people and their senatorial leaders was not to be overcome. Carthage was finally and utterly destroyed in the 607th year from the foundation of Rome, a little under 450 years ago. It was at this time that Rome also destroyed the city of Corinth in Greece, and a little later the city of Numantia in Spain.

The defeat of her great enemy, Carthage, and the destruction of great cities may have resulted in hubris and the moral decay of the Republic, turning the goddess Fortuna against Rome. Certainly, booty flowed into the city and with it came ideas from the Greek East, new luxuries, and the creation of an economy based on slavery. Major changes followed:

*The gifted General Lucius Cornelius Sulla marched on Rome twice and held several important offices of state, declaring himself dictator and twice being consul of the Roman Republic.*

## THE URBAN PLEBS

Originally, the inhabitants of the city itself were the junior partners in the state. The urban plebs were all registered in four voting tribes, whereas their rural counterparts were spread over the other 31 voting tribes. The urban plebs lacked property and were discriminated against, voting last in elections of the Comitia Centuriata that decided weighty matters such as war and peace, and the election of the consuls.

All this was to change with the rise of Publius Clodius. He gave the urban plebs, all 320,000 of them, free corn and organized them on a quasi-military basis to disrupt the workings of the state, including elections, with riots. The aristocrats hired gladiators to combat violence with violence, and Clodius was killed at an inn on the Appian Way. The plebs cremated his body in the forum and at the same time burnt down the Senate house.

Today, 360 years later, the urban plebs still receive the free distribution of grain established by Clodius—the Roman plebs must be one of the most numerous and privileged groups of people in the entire empire.

the army ceased to be composed of property-holding citizens and instead began to include members of the working class, the urban *plebs*. As a consequence, these soldiers, now trained by the professional instructors of gladiators, were loyal only to their commander.

The army of General Sulla became the first Roman army to march on Rome, crushing all opposition and establishing Sulla as dictator—a post that he later resigned. His legacy was to establish a new age of military power held in the hands of Pompey, Caesar, and Crassus, and causing those who held the consulships to become either their lackeys or men who achieved little in their year of office.

# HISTORY: FROM JULIUS CAESAR TO CAESAR AUGUSTUS

IN THE 704TH YEAR OF THE CITY'S HISTORY, SOME 348 YEARS AGO, JULIUS CAESAR CROSSED THE RIVER RUBICON AND ENTERED ITALY WITH HIS ARMY. MANY ROMANS TURNED TO POMPEY, WHO DREW UP HIS FORCES, AND THERE BEGAN A PERIOD OF ALMOST TWENTY YEARS OF CIVIL WAR, FOUGHT IN SPAIN, NORTH AFRICA, GREECE, EGYPT, AND EVEN IN ITALY ITSELF. CAESAR DEFEATED POMPEY, SETTING HIMSELF UP AS DICTATOR FOR LIFE, ONLY TO BE MURDERED BY A LARGE GROUP OF SENATORS BEFORE A STATUE OF POMPEY SOME FIVE YEARS LATER.

The conspirators had no plan beyond the murder. Mark Anthony, caesar's second in command, emerged as the leader of the Caesarian party, while Octavian—the nineteen-year-old grandnephew and heir of caesar—raised an army of his adopted father's veterans and formed an alliance with Anthony to revenge caesar's death.

Vengeance was duly gained at the Battle of Philippi, where 100,000 Roman soldiers were ranged against each other. However, hardly had the victory celebrations been concluded when Anthony and Octavian fell out and there ensued a second battle for the Roman world.

Anthony marshaled the forces of the East against those of the West, commanded by Agrippa on behalf of Octavian. This time a naval battle at Actium was decisive; the East fell to caesar's heir, and Rome appropriated all the wealth of the kingdom of Egypt. No opposition now existed to Octavian, who held absolute power over the whole of the Roman world at just 32.

### THE AUGUSTAN EMPIRE

Octavian returned to Rome victorious and began a policy of renewal. Some 82 temples were restored, the Senate was purged, and the republic was declared to have been restored. Octavian was awarded the title Augustus, given a personal bodyguard, and retained the right to appoint the commanders of the 28 legions stationed at the empire's frontiers.

There may have been elections and meetings of the Senate, but

*The emperor Augustus, who claimed to restore the republic, although in reality he established the Roman Empire.*

WHAT TO EXPECT

## SENATORS

Today, senators are detached from the heart of power, which can be found closer to the frontiers in the emperors' palaces. The Senate performs what can only be described as a ceremonial function. However, there was a time when the emperor had to request the Senate's permission and even Vespasian had to listen to lengthy speeches criticizing not just his policies, but even his pronunciation.

The processions of senators with their toga-clad followers snaking their way through the city from their homes to the Curia (senate house) in the old forum are a spectacle that can be seen after the second hour of the day, and should not be missed by visitors to the city.

power now rested firmly with the emperor and his court. The city was rebuilt and clad in marble, and this legacy can still be seen by visitors to the Temple of Apollo on the Palatine Hill.

Augustus was a mild man; he wished to be called *princeps* or first amongst equals, rather than *dominus* or lord—something that some of his successors did not hold with. His long reign established a system of government, a set of conservative morals, a religious basis, and the financial structure to pay a regular army.

Augustus' successors (Tiberius, Caligula, Claudius, and Nero) were far from perfect; but the system endured. Even after a year of civil war and the new Flavian dynasty, little seemed to change. Indeed, it is as though the empire simply became stronger, culminating in the reign of Trajan when the largest area of Roman rule was established not just to the west, but also north of the Danube, and east across the Euphrates.

# History: The Modern Empire

Rome dominates an empire stretching from the ocean in the west to the River Euphrates in the east, and from Caledonia in the north to the upper reaches of the River Nile in the south. The emperor Hadrian and his successors sought to establish some sort of logic to the boundaries of the empire. Rivers formed natural frontiers in the Rhine, the Danube and the Euphrates. Elsewhere, artificial boundaries were created: in the north of Britannia a garrisoned wall was constructed; and in the semi-desert of North Africa a series of fortified settlements were established to control water resources.

It is at the frontiers that soldiers are stationed to ensure, at least in theory, that they will be able to mobilize quickly against any threat from the barbarians. The system worked well from the time of Augustus through to that of Marcus Aurelius, but in the more recent past small barbarian nations have begun to form larger alliances, and Rome now faces some formidable enemies: the Franks, the Alemanni, the Goths, and a resurgent Persian Empire under the Sassanians.

These peoples not only threaten the provinces, but Italy itself—only 30 years ago the emperor Aurelian fought off some kinsmen of the Alemanni in two battles in northern Italy. It was around this time that Gaul, Greece, the Balkan provinces, and parts of Asia Minor were invaded by large barbarian groups and the province of Dacia had to be evacuated. Happily, in the last 20 years, much has been done to make amends, and Rome's new rulers appear to have the barbarian threat under control.

## THE ARMY, CIVILIANS, AND THE EMPERORS

The consequences of the barbarian threats that first developed 60 or 70 years ago were that emperors needed to be near the frontiers and required money to pay their troops on campaign. Many emperors, in need of cash, simply reduced the silver and gold content of the coinage—effectively making enough coins to pay their soldiers, but decreasing their actual value. Civilians have felt the cost of a devalued coinage: an overall rise in prices. Indeed, it has become difficult to persuade the local aristocracies to pay for the restoration of temples, theaters, and amphitheaters in many of the cities of the empire.

Most Romans hope that the introduction of maximum prices and wages will curb inflation—now realized to be a negative effect of the debasement of the coinage.

This volatility was exacerbated by a tendency for generals to be proclaimed emperors and then march on Rome, or move against the nearest army under the command of a rival claimant.

Romans now recognize the need for a permanent army in the field, ready to take on an invader, and that the emperor or emperors need to be stationed near the frontiers. Hence, power now lies in Maximian's palace in Mediolanum (Milan) rather than the Senate house in the old forum in Rome.

*Entrance to a Roman fortress—note that a civilian settlement has grown up around the fortress.*

# POLITICS: THE EMPIRE TODAY

SIXTEEN YEARS AGO, DIOCLETIAN WAS CHOSEN AS RULER BY THE SOLDIERS IN NICOMEDIA. HE SUCCESSFULLY TOOK OVER THE GOVERNMENT OF THE EMPIRE AND TWO YEARS LATER APPOINTED MAXIMIAN, A FORMER COMRADE IN ARMS, AS HIS JOINT RULER IN THE WEST. THIS IS A NEW SYSTEM OF GOVERNMENT, IN WHICH THERE ARE IN EFFECT TWO EMPERORS, EACH HOLDING THE TITLE AUGUSTUS.

Rome's rulers are no longer aristocrats, but provincials of low birth who have risen through the ranks of the army. Diocletian was born in Dalmatia into a peasant family, while Maximian was also born of peasant stock from Sirmium. Both men rose to positions of power during their service in the army.

Diocletian possesses a genius for organization—no area of the empire's troubles has escaped his attention, and he has devised a new system of government. Meanwhile, Maximian has restored Rome itself after the great fire some 15 years ago—there is a new Curia for the Senate to meet in, and he has initiated a project for a set of baths larger even than those of Caracalla.

Both Diocletian and Maximian have their deputies, recognized by the title caesar and adopted as their respective heirs (Maximian's biological son will not inherit the throne). Today, Rome has four rulers in what is becoming known as the Tetrarchy. Constantius, the caesar of the West, is married to Theodora the daughter of Maximian, and has had great success in recovering the province of Britannia for the Romans, after it had been seized by Carausius.

## THE FUTURE OF THE TETRARCHY

There are rumors that an impending persecution of Christians is planned—neither Diocletian nor Maximian hold with new religions, and both prefer the older traditions of Roman paganism—so travelers are well advised to keep their religious views to themselves.

Another popular rumor is that in five years' time, both Diocletian and Maximian will retire into private life—a rumor that is bolstered by the building of what may well become Diocletian's retirement home in Spalatum (Split). If they do retire, the respective caesars in the East and West will assume control.

Their legacy will be a rejection of hereditary succession, seeing the appointment of two men ruling as brothers with equal authority over a unified empire. To depose of one would result in the vengeance of the other, and the stability of this system should be a vast improvement on the period of chaos that followed the death of Septimius Severus, which saw 35 or more emperors and usurpers in just 73 years.

Romans now hope for a future in which Rome once again holds sway over all her former territories, perhaps even Dacia, abandoned 30 years ago to the barbarians.

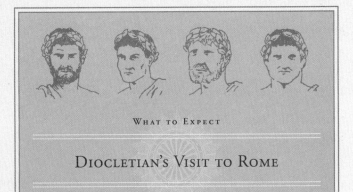

WHAT TO EXPECT

## DIOCLETIAN'S VISIT TO ROME

In November Anno 309 (1055 years from Romulus' foundation of the city) the tetrarchs are due to visit Rome to celebrate the twentieth year of the rule of Diocletian. There will be a triumphal procession, and a new triumphal arch is already under construction.

Previous celebrations, such as those held in Mediolanum nine years ago, saw the Senate present, and speeches of praise given by the best orators, who alluded to Diocletian as Jupiter, and Maximian as Hercules, righting the wrongs of our age. A map showing all the regions in which military successes have been attained is also under construction.

The events will also be a time of religious celebration and an opportunity for the reassertion of Rome's pagan traditions. Rome will be full of visitors, so it is suggested that you make arrangements for both transport and accommodation as soon as possible.

# PEOPLE: THE POPULATION OF ROME

WHO ARE THE ROMANS? ETHNICITIES ARE OFTEN DIFFICULT TO PIN DOWN, AND THE ROMANS ARE NO EXCEPTION. FOR A LONG TIME, THEY DEFINED THEMSELVES AS CULTURALLY OPPOSITE TO THE GREEKS OR THE BARBARIANS. THEY MADE MUCH OF THE ISSUE OF THEIR ROMAN CITIZENSHIP, AS OPPOSED TO ALL BUT THE PROVINCIAL ELITE'S LACK OF ENFRANCHISEMENT. HOWEVER, FOR NEARLY A CENTURY NOW ALL FREE INHABITANTS OF THE ROMAN EMPIRE HAVE BEEN CLASSIFIED AS ROMAN CITIZENS.

**THE PEOPLES OF ITALY** Following the Social War, almost 400 years ago, between Rome and her Italian allies, the free peoples of Italy were granted Roman citizenship and enrolled in the voting tribes at Rome. However, this did not mean that all Italians saw themselves simply as Romans. For example, Cicero regarded every Italian as having two homelands: Rome and the city of his birth, in Cicero's case Arpinum. Hence, another famous senator, Pliny, had a home city in Como in northern Italy, but his other home city was

## ROMAN CITIZENSHIP

Today, everyone in the Roman Empire who is free is a citizen. However, in the past, the number of citizens was much smaller and other Italians only became citizens of Rome some 670 years after its foundation—in fact they went to war with Rome over citizenship. Interestingly, freed slaves have become citizens from very early on in Rome's history, as did veteran soldiers recruited from non-citizens resident in the provinces.

The emperor Caracalla granted the citizenship to all free persons 88 years ago, and today there are 60 million tax-paying citizens.

Rome. The visitor will be faced with some confusion over the place and geography of ethnic divisions within Italy. Today there are nine administrative regions: the Cottian Alps; Venetia and Histria; Aemilia and Liguria; Flaminia and Picenum; Tuscia and Umbria; Campania; Apulia and Calabria; and finally Lucania and Brutium.

Close to Rome, you will find the cities of Rome's Latin allies. These have a similar culture to that of Rome in the time of the early republic. This is the land of the famous Caecuban wines, and is very fertile. The city of Ardea, with the nearby ancient sanctuary of Venus, is probably the best town to visit if you want to see a truly ancient Latin city.

To the north of Rome lie the Etruscan and Sabine ethnic groups, the former characterized by their ancient language—seldom used today and spoken only by a few people who preserve the tongue. (The emperor Claudius' book on the Etruscans is a mine of information.) Sutri is the Etruscan city closest to Rome, where you can see the tombs and their contents: pots, armor, and some writings are the only surviving monuments of this ancient culture today. The Sabines, so integral to the story of Rome's foundation, continue to inhabit a region that virtually lacks

cities, with the people only coming together for markets that coincide with the shipment, on the hoof, of sheep and mules to Rome. The biannual markets at Forum Novum (hardly a city at all) are the place to meet these rustic people.

For those wishing to see the Samnite country, stout boots will be required. These famous opponents of Rome live in the mountains southeast of Rome. Their ancient armor is well known to all who visit the gladiatorial contests and have seen the Samnite gladiators fight (see pp.104–5).

## TOTA ITALIA

These ethnicities are very difficult to identify today; the distinctions of dress, language, and weaponry that were reported by the Greek geographer Strabo some 300 years ago have fallen away. But still the population persists in using these ancient distinctions to maintain a cultural divide between themselves and others. Hence, you will find in the cities of the south that many will refer to themselves as part of Magna Graecia, even though, apart from Naples, there is little by way of Greek dress, language, or cultural institutions on display. A visitor might even conclude that the idea of a unified Italy, "tota Italia," lies only in the imagination of its inhabitants and their rulers.

## PEOPLES OF THE WEST

From the time of the sack of Rome by the Gauls, 363 years after the city had been founded, the Romans have had a powerful and longlasting fear that their city might once again be destroyed by the peoples of the north. However, we find in the records that Cicero, the eminent orator of the past, was taught by a Gaul—one Marcus Antonius Gnipho—even before Julius Caesar had conquered the three Gauls.

What this suggests is that Gauls have migrated to Rome from much earlier times and some have been living in the city for generations.

Today, you will find numerous traders in Rome and representatives of the shippers who transport supplies up the River Rhône

*Septimius Severus came from Leptis Magna in Africa. He was hailed as emperor by his soldiers, when news reached the frontiers that Pertinax had been murdered. His home city greatly benefited from his patronage, with much redevelopment of the civic center.*

onward to the Saône and to the armies in the two provinces of Germany. There are rather good textiles and clothing made by the Gauls on sale in Rome.

Spaniards are abundant in the city, although less so than previously since the olive oil distributed to the urban plebs is now sourced from Africa rather than Spain; but you will still see them selling olive oil, garum, and other goods in the emporium or river port close to the Aventine.

Many are cultured, and you may already know some of the great Spanish authors, whose Latin works are quite famous: Columella on agriculture; Martial with his witty epigrams; and Quintilian, whose handbook on oratory and rhetoric is required reading for all would-be public speakers.

It is worth noting that both the emperors Trajan and Hadrian hailed from Spain, and you will find in their native place, Italica, an enormous temple dedicated to Trajan—however, much of the new city designed, or at least paid for, by Hadrian is gradually being abandoned.

There are few Britons in Rome, but do ask the local magistrates if any are resident. You can, however, see British charioteers and gladiators in the circus and amphitheater, alongside Lusitanians, Spaniards, and Gauls.

## AFRICANS

Over the last century, ever since Septimius Severus was emperor, the number of Africans in the Roman Senate has increased; now as many as one in eight is from Africa. But scribes, lawyers, jurists, traders, and charioteers have also made their way to Rome. Some describe themselves as Punic, others as Libyan, and some as Numidians, or even Mauretanians. All are well-connected, with various interest groups in the city—most obviously the corporations of shippers and traders in grain and oil, with their links to the prefect of the corn and oil distributions to the people.

You will find these people in the trading districts of Rome, close to the river, and also in Ostia and Portus. It would seem that in recent times, the North African provinces have not suffered from the economic dislocation or the political upheavals that have characterized the recent history of Gaul, Spain, and some of the eastern provinces.

Anyone wishing to witness this for themselves should take a ship from Portus for the short trip to Carthage or Leptis Magna (see pp.96–7), the home city of the emperors Septimius Severus and Caracalla. You will certainly conclude that both Africa and Africans have a large role to play in modern Rome.

## PEOPLES OF THE EAST

The Romans have embraced the culture of Greece with a passion. They may have conquered Greece itself, but Greek culture seems to have conquered them.

In Rome you may find Greek instructors in rhetoric, philosophy, and grammar, all for hire. There is also a vast number of architects, astronomers, and astrologers—many coming from Alexandria in Egypt, rather than the from the ancient center of learning at Athens in Greece—while medicine continues to be dominated by the Greek legacy.

Greek culture can be viewed at the shrine of Dionysius, established 150 years ago by Pompeia Agrippinilla—a migrant from the island of Lesbos—to which many of the Greek population continue to flock.

Greeks from the cities of Asia Minor often appear in Rome as ambassadors from their home cities, with a view to settling some trivial dispute or other.

There are many Syrians in Rome; some are traders and others soldiers. The best place to meet them is at the Syrian Sanctuary across the Tiber on the Janiculum Hill—almost exclusively used by the Syrian workers of Transtiberim and in the warehouses of the river port, known as the Horrea Galbiana. Nearby is the sanctuary of the Sun God where many Palmyrenes worship.

## EGYPT IN ROME

Some 300 years ago, the defeat of Cleopatra and Anthony led to the conquest of Egypt by the future emperor Augustus. This was marked by wholesale looting, and from its conquest Egypt was placed under the direct rule of the emperor; the province now provides a vast amount of the grain distributed to the plebs in Rome.

Egyptomania seems to have taken a strong hold on Roman culture: some wealthy Romans even construct their tombs in the form of a pyramid.

You will find that most Egyptians in Rome are in fact either Greeks or Jews from Alexandria rather than ethnic Egyptians. All tend to favor the Greek language, and the only hieroglyphs that you will see in Rome are those found on booty brought back by the emperor Augustus.

Egyptians are to be found in the vicus of Isis and Serapis, but not all the worshippers of these gods are Alexandrians or their descendants. For further information, ask to see the Prophetes or Pater at any temple of Serapis or Isis.

## THE JEWS OF ROME

There have been Jews in Rome for over 400 years, and the first may have been slaves traded across the Mediterranean. A steady flow of Jewish migrants has continued, often with Diaspora Jews sold into slavery. Their numbers increased substantially after the suppression of revolts in Judaea and later insurrections on the part of other Diaspora Jews in Egypt and North Africa. There are probably 40,000 Jews resident in Rome today.

The Jews have far greater coherence than many other groups because of their ancient belief in a single god and their use of the Hebrew language. There are numerous synagogues in the city, and Rome's Jews have played an important role in the development of Jewish customs; including the Hebrew scholar Todos, who is responsible for the practice of eating a young goat or lamb at Passover. The Romans are tolerant of the Jews and respect their ancient religion, even though the emperor Titus destroyed their temple in Jerusalem and imposed a Jewish tax.

*An obelisk from Egypt looted by the emperor Augustus and transported to Rome, where it became the pointer on his vast sundial—its subsidence meant that it ceased to be accurate within 50 years.*

# RELIGION: NEW VERSUS OLD

IN ROME THE RELIGIOUS SITUATION IS TENSE. MOST ROMANS
BELIEVE VERY STRONGLY THAT THE IMMORTAL GODS CREATED
THE WORLD, AND THAT THEIR WORSHIP SHOULD CONTINUE IN
THE SAME MANNER IN WHICH IT HAS BEEN CONDUCTED FOR
GENERATIONS. YET THE FOLLOWERS OF THE NEW RELIGION
OF CHRISTIANITY ARE INCREASING IN NUMBER AND BECOMING
BETTER ORGANIZED. MANY THINK THAT A NEW RELIGIOUS
CONFLICT, SUCH AS THOSE OF THE PAST, IS IMMINENT.

To abandon the religious practices of their forefathers is simply unthinkable to most Romans; and to switch religions, in the view of Diocletian and others, would be the height of criminality.

In Rome you may see hundreds of temples to many different gods, and hardly a day goes by without a festival being celebrated. The mainstay of the Roman belief system is the maintenance of the benign favor of the gods. This is secured via sacrifices of bulls, boars, and rams; offerings of food; the pouring of libations; and the burning of incense. There are also prayers, but the main thing is that the rituals should be performed as they always have been.

Roman gods are not so different from humans—if you believe the stories about them. They bicker and fight, fall in love, have a lot of sex, and also direct the lives of humans.

*The sacrifice of animals plays an important part in many of Rome's religious ceremonies, helping to secure the favor of the gods.*

Perhaps it is no surprise that many of Rome's more powerful emperors have also become gods.

## A NEW RELIGION

It is unsurprising that Christians are so unpopular in Rome. They insist that no other god exists apart from their own, and stubbornly refuse to offer even a little incense to the emperor and his family. They have even suggested that the Roman gods are in fact some sort of evil demons.

What many Christians seem to seek is martyrdom. Many governors in the provinces, when presented with Christians, have provided every opportunity for them to conform with the most basic requirements of

the state—an offering of incense to the emperor's genius, for example—but have often been rebuffed with repeated statements of faith. In the end the governors have reluctantly had to expose these fanatics to the beasts and martyrdom. Perhaps this is what makes the religion of Christianity so attractive to some; after all, they follow the teachings of a miracle worker who was himself crucified as a criminal.

There is a number of newly built churches to the Christian god, and Rome has a Christian community that is less fundamentalist than others. Their bishop, Marcellinus, is even rumored to have made sacrifices to the immortal gods, despite remaining a Christian. Most Christians expect the return of their Messiah imminently, and seek to live a good life—even if that means rejecting the authority of the emperors.

Many today have urged Diocletian to take on the Christians: to destroy their churches; exclude them from the baths and other public buildings of the cities of the empire; exclude them from legal redress (in effect permitting anyone to assault them); and for their sacred books to be burnt. It should be noted, though, that the number of Christians in the empire is increasing, and this threat of persecution does little to dissuade them from their beliefs.

# DOMESTIC LIFE: THE ROLE OF THE FAMILY

FOR CICERO, THAT GREAT ORATOR OF THE PAST, THE FAMILY WAS THE BUILDING BLOCK OF THE STATE. IT IS AN INSTITUTION THAT WAS DELINEATED AND REGULATED BY ROMULUS ALL THOSE YEARS AGO, AND IS STILL REVERED BY MOST ROMANS, WHETHER BORN FREE OR INTO SLAVERY.

Relationships within families are characterized by piety. Fathers, although they may have an almost tyrannical legal power over their sons and daughters, try to create a relationship of respect between their children and themselves.

Just as there is respect between children and fathers, there is a deep reverence for ancestors, and in many of the larger houses you will see their wax facemasks in the household shrines, and sometimes even family trees.

## MARRIAGE

Roman marriage is based on the consent of the fathers or guardians of bride and of the groom, as well as the couple themselves.

It is legal for women to be married from the age of 12 and men from the age of 14; but in practice girls are generally married off in their mid-to-late teens and men in their mid-to-late twenties. Prior to marriage, the girl is given gifts by her husband, which include an engagement ring. Fathers of girls

*Although the institution of marriage places the man at the head of the family, women retain a degree of independent power.*

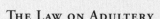

## THE LAW ON ADULTERY

In the laws of Rome a married woman who has sex with a man who is not her husband is considered an adulteress. If she is caught in the act, the husband or father of the woman has the right to kill the adulterer.

Such adultery usually results in divorce, but it is not considered adultery for a husband to be unfaithful, as long as his partners are neither virgins nor married to another man. This allows for sex with the slaves of a household and also with prostitutes.

Some regard this as a sign of the patriarchal bias of Roman society, while others suggest that the law reflects a way in which a man may limit the number of his wife's pregnancies, sparing her from the traumas of childbirth.

need to provide a dowry and try to locate a promising future husband by the time their daughter is ten years old.

Successful marriages produce children, and those that are childless normally end in divorce. The procedure for divorce is simple, but does involve the return of the dowry. Both husband and wife own property separately, so that it is necessary to maintain clear accounts of who owns what.

Augustus introduced incentives for the upper classes to marry and have children, and it is now expected that all good citizens become parents. Many Romans marry more than once, often due to death or divorce. All Roman men below the age of 60 and all Roman women below the age of 50 tend to be married.

## WOMEN IN SOCIETY

Although women have few civic rights, they can own property and hold some considerable power. As they are usually younger than their husbands, most can expect to be widowed in later life. It is at this time that they can wield considerable influence over their sons' and daughters' actions.

The most powerful woman in Rome's history may have been Cornelia, the mother of the Gracchi: two young men who were murdered by their fellow senators for not only suggesting the poor should have a greater stake in the republic, but also taking action to alleviate the exploitation of the poor by the rich. After their murder, she continued to regale the visitors to her villa with tales of her sons or her "two jewels."

# AGRICULTURE AND INDUSTRY: TRADE IN THE EMPIRE

THE PRODUCE OF THE LAND, THE SEA, AND THE RIVERS OF ALL THE PARTS OF THE EMPIRE ARE BROUGHT TO ROME. NOWHERE ELSE WILL YOU SEE SUCH AN ABUNDANCE OF ALL THAT IS GROWN OR MANUFACTURED. THE ARRIVALS AND DEPARTURES OF SHIPS IN PORTUS ARE UNCEASING. IF YOU CANNOT FIND A PRODUCT IN ROME, CHANCES ARE THAT IT SIMPLY DOES NOT EXIST.

### AGRICULTURE

There are two major markets for goods in the Roman Empire: the city of Rome and the armies on the frontiers. To supply these two concentrations of population with food and goods, a complicated network of trade has been established.

The flow of goods to Rome is in itself impressive—Italian agriculture alone cannot support the urban population. Instead, for more than 400 years, grain and oil have been imported by sea from Africa, Egypt, Spain, and Sicily. Transport is undertaken by private individuals, but for the supply of *annona* (the free corn and oil distributions to the plebs) the contract is held with the state. The same private individuals have made it their business to become involved in the supply of food to the soldiers. Olives and grapes do not grow in the northern parts of the empire, but those products that can be preserved for long enough to ship over long distances are the ones that will make the traders, if not the producers, rich. Livestock transported on the hoof to Rome commands a good price too, not to mention the white bulls bred in Umbria for sacrifice to the gods.

### INDUSTRY

Manufacturing in the Roman Empire is based in the workshop rather than the factory. Labor is normally supplied by men and beasts—although there are also some very impressive examples of the use of water power for the milling of grain.

Some experiments have been undertaken into the use of steam power, but these have proven both costly and dangerous—and with abundant human resources, including slaves, few want to

*Portus was constructed under the emperor Claudius and then expanded under Trajan. It is the largest artificial harbor in the Mediterranean.*

conduct any further investigation into this frightening technology.

Although lacking factories, the level of manufacture across the empire should not be underestimated. Goods carried in amphorae from as far south as Africa can be found for sale in Britannia in the distant north. At the same time, no one should underestimate the level of trade at a local level supporting the numerous cities of the empire.

### MINING

The Romans have extracted more materials from the earth than any other people in history. They have mined not just building materials and beautiful rocks, but also metals. You will perhaps be surprised to learn that the worst punishment the Romans can inflict on a criminal is not exposure to the beasts, nor indeed crucifixion, but condemnation to the mines.

Whatever is being quarried, the work is hard; for those who are sent to copper, lead, silver, or gold mines, life is short, and even the overseers and mine managers frequently become sick.

Parts of the provinces are scarred with gashes from which the earth's minerals are extracted, and in many places few crops will grow due to the mining and smelting of ores.

# WARFARE AND THE ARMY

SOLDIERS, LED BY THE EMPERORS, ESSENTIALLY ACT AS THE GUARD OF THE FLOCK OF INHABITANTS WHO LIVE WITHIN THE EMPIRE. SOLDIERS SERVE FOR A TERM OF 20 YEARS, AND ROME HAS HAD A PROFESSIONAL ARMY PAID FOR BY TAXATION SINCE THE TIME OF AUGUSTUS.

The last 120 years have seen more warfare, with a greater impact on the people of the empire, than the previous two centuries. Barbarians have invaded not just the frontier regions, but the heart of the empire, even Italy itself. At the same time, uncertainties over the succession and the ambitions of usurpers have placed the empire in danger, with soldiers leaving the frontiers to fight civil wars in the hope that their commander might come to rule.

Politics is backed by military force, and the emperor Septimius

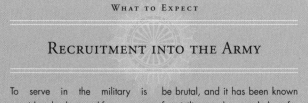

WHAT TO EXPECT

## RECRUITMENT INTO THE ARMY

To serve in the military is considered to be good for a young man. Twenty years after joining up, if he survives, he may return to civilian life and will find that his veteran status is advantageous and exempts him from a large number of obligations, including that of taxation. Conscription can be brutal, and it has been known for civilians to be rounded up for service. There have even been cases of able-bodied men mutilating themselves to avoid service. Both pagans and Christians serve in the army, but some Christians have been punished for their refusal to fight in the name of the emperors.

Severus' advice to his son to "Pay the army and ignore everybody else" has become the byword of his successors. This is not a new phenomenon—Augustus was the first to pay his bodyguard double wages—but it was in later times that usurpers hurried to the barracks of the praetorians, where the position of emperor was essentially available to the highest bidder.

When Rome has succumbed to civil war in the past, the new emperor's soldiers were generally recruited from far away; these were ferocious to look at, terrifying to hear, and coarse in conversation. Romans have lived through some dangerous times, but with Diocletian and Maximian now at the helm, the future looks secure.

## THE MODERN ARMY

It may seem strange that, for the best part of the last 250 years, the soldiers in the army have not been recruited from Italy. Another more recent change is that senators are no longer the only people who can command a legion. There are plenty of commanders drawn from the *equites* (Roman knights).

The fact that the empire is ruled by four men in a tetrarchy creates a system of four commanders. The need to have a larger number of soldiers stationed on the frontiers in fortresses and four major armies permanently in the field has caused an overall reduction in the number of farmers in many areas. The empire also struggles to provide money via taxes to support this increase in military power; even Italy and Rome are now subject to taxation, something that was previously abolished more than 450 years ago.

*Roman soldiers depend upon a shield, a helmet, and chain-mail for their defense, using a spear and a sword to attack with.*

# THE CITY
# OF ROME

*Wherever you turn in Rome you will see
a crowded display of wonderful sights. It is virtually
impossible to take all these in during a single visit,
so you need to decide which of these marvels hold the
most interest for you and will provide the most
enduring memories of this great city.*

# THE LARGEST CITY ON EARTH

ROME HAS A POPULATION OF OVER A MILLION INHABITANTS, WHO LIVE IN 46,000 APARTMENT BLOCKS AND OVER 1,700 HIGH-CLASS HOUSES THAT ARE DISTRIBUTED ACROSS ITS 424 NEIGHBORHOODS.

Rome is a clean city: there are more than 800 public baths served with fresh water from 19 aqueducts. The latter also provide people with fresh drinking water delivered to them at the many street fountains—some 352 in total.

The streets are paved and, for the most part, well maintained, with eight bridges traversing the River Tiber. The recently constructed city walls stretch for some 20 miles in circumference, and there are 37 impressive gates.

There is something for everyone within this vast metropolis: from the scholarly delights of the 28 libraries, to the more corporeal pleasures of the 46 official brothels—far more if you count the unofficial ones—Rome caters to every taste.

## THE STREETS OF ROME

Because Rome is built on seven hills, you will find that the streets in the valleys between them form the major routes through the city. Most of these lead from one of the major gates to the golden milestone, next to the victory arch of Septimius Severus in the old forum. The major routes or *viae*—for example, the Via Lata—have been constructed so that processions into the city can take place. The viae are much wider than the lesser streets called *vici*—confusingly the same word that the Romans use for a neighborhood.

The viae, although they often contain more traffic, tend to flow at a much faster speed than the vici, and after dark the viae are far safer than the narrow alleyways of the city.

Almost all of the streets are paved in a black stone that is particularly durable. It is quarried near Rome and must have been formed when one or more volcanoes erupted in those times before Hercules had defeated the Giants (who are said today to reside in the earth beneath volcanoes).

*Many of Rome's streets are narrow, while the buildings that flank them can rise as high as 60 Roman feet.*

# AN OVERVIEW OF THE CITY

SO MUCH TO SEE, SO LITTLE TIME TO SEE IT IN. ROME IS A CITY THAT HAS IT ALL, AND IS SO RESPLENDENT THAT IN MODERN TIMES IT EVEN ECLIPSES THE CITY OF MARBLE MONUMENTS CONSTRUCTED BY AUGUSTUS SOME 300 YEARS AGO. HOWEVER, IN A CITY OF SO MANY WONDROUS SIGHTS THE VISITOR IS POSED WITH THE QUESTION OF WHERE TO START AND WHAT TO SEE FIRST.

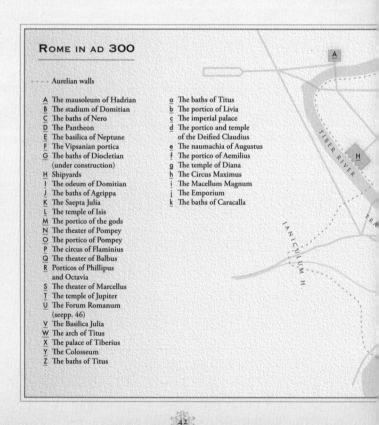

## ROME IN AD 300

- - - - Aurelian walls

A  The mausoleum of Hadrian
B  The stadium of Domitian
C  The baths of Nero
D  The Pantheon
E  The basilica of Neptune
F  The Vipsanian portica
G  The baths of Diocletian
    (under construction)
H  Shipyards
I  The odeum of Domitian
J  The baths of Agrippa
K  The Saepta Julia
L  The temple of Isis
M  The portico of the gods
N  The theater of Pompey
O  The portico of Pompey
P  The circus of Flaminius
Q  The theater of Balbus
R  Porticos of Phillipus
    and Octavia
S  The theater of Marcellus
T  The temple of Jupiter
U  The Forum Romanum
    (seepp. 46)
V  The Basilica Julia
W  The arch of Titus
X  The palace of Tiberius
Y  The Colosseum
Z  The baths of Titus

a  The baths of Titus
b  The portico of Livia
c  The imperial palace
d  The portico and temple
    of the Deified Claudius
e  The naumachia of Augustus
f  The portico of Aemilius
g  The temple of Diana
h  The Circus Maximus
i  The Macellum Magnum
j  The Emporium
k  The baths of Caracalla

TIBER RIVER

JANICULUM H.

## REBUILDING ROME

The great fire of 17 years ago did much damage and destroyed a substantial part of the city, including the old forum, the Curia, the forum of Julius Caesar, and much of the Basilica Julia. The people of Rome, though, are fortunate that Diocletian and Maximian have attended to the work of renewal that has included not just these monuments, but also the theater of Pompey, the temple of Isis and Serapis in the Campus Martius, and the baths of Diocletian. The scale of the works undertaken has caused brick-making to become, once again, a boom industry in the vicinity of Rome.

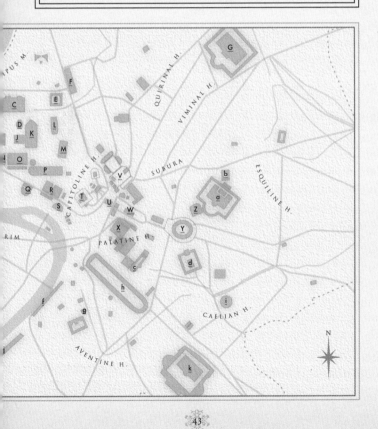

# THE HISTORIC CENTER

THE ANCIENTS REGARDED CIVIC VIRTUE AS EXISTING IN THE
FORUM, AND THIS FEELING IS ENHANCED TODAY BY THE
PRESENCE OF THE TEMPLES OF THE DIVINE EMPERORS AT
THE HISTORIC CENTER OF ROME.

Ask your litter bearers to drop you off at the Meta Sudans, the fountain at the end of the Via Sacra. From here proceed past the temple of Venus and Rome, and the Templum Urbis or City Temple, all of which are being restored after the fire of 17 years ago.

Continue up the hill to the triumphal arch of Titus that celebrates his victory over the Jews and the destruction of the Jewish temple in Jerusaleum. There is a good view of the palaces that bestride the Palatine Hill, and to your left you will see the venerable temple of Jupiter Stator. Compared to the temple of Venus and Rome, it is a small structure, but its antiquity alone makes it well worth a visit.

As you pass along the street, you will see numerous statues of the emperors, and it is well worth reading the inscriptions to see who has paid for these dedications.

Continuing down the Via Sacra, you pass the residence of the Vestal Virgins, rebuilt by Septimius Severus; you should then visit the circular temple of Venus. This is where the Vestals keep the eternal fire alight, and might be described as the sacred hearth of Rome. Adjacent to the temple of Venus, you will see a small dwelling: the Regia, where the ancient kings of Rome resided prior to the foundation of the republic.

Rising up above this structure is the magnificent temple dedicated to Faustina, the wife of Antoninus Pius, who was deified at her death. During her life she had not only been a chaste wife, but had also supported young, poor girls.

### THE OLD FORUM

On entering the forum, you will be met by an array of sights evocative of historical events decided upon in the Curia or senate house. To your left lies the temple of Julius Caesar, in front of which is a new platform or *rostra* surmounted by columns with images of the gods, where public speeches are made.

The forum has been subject to reconstruction in recent years, since it was severely damaged by fire, and the result is a rather splendid modern space. To the left of the forum you will see the ancient temple of Castor and Pollux, although the structure is mostly the result of work carried out by Tiberius in the reign of Augustus, and it is a classic example of the use of white marble of that time.

Moving toward the Capitoline, still on the left of the forum, the Basilica Julia has been recently rebuilt, and seven columns each bearing a deity have been placed in front. This has created a more defined central area to the forum, which will be enhanced when the new rostra is completed.

Entering the Basilica Julia, originally built by Julius Caesar and Augustus, you will be astounded by the vast covered space. If it is raining or unpleasantly hot, it may be crowded with traders, senators, children, and others at play. Gaming boards have been scratched into the pavement, and you will find numerous expert players taking on all comers.

From here, cross the forum to the Basilica Paulli, which is faced with a series of offices. Though smaller than the Basilica Julia it is of greater antiquity, and most of what you can see dates to the Augustan period. Notice several historical friezes.

Leaving the Basilica, walk toward the Curia; you will encounter a square of black stone on which it is forbidden to walk. It was here that Romulus disappeared, never

*Recent additions to the Forum Romanum include the statues on the columns—Jupiter is on the tallest one—in front of the Basilica Julia.*

to be seen again.

It is a short walk to the new Curia where the senate meets. If it is in session (once a month), you will see a crowd of hangers-on outside, who will be happy to pass on rumors and gossip of the debates within.

Next to the Curia is the arch of Septimius Severus that celebrates his victories over the barbarians. Next to this is the rostra of Augustus.

*The arch of Septimius Severus depicts defeated enemies and victorious Romans.*

# THE IMPERIAL FORA

THE FOUR FORA BUILT BY JULIUS CAESAR, AUGUSTUS,
DOMITIAN AND NERVA, AND TRAJAN PROVIDE THE CITY WITH
SPACE FOR THE ADMINISTRATION OF PUBLIC AFFAIRS. THE
ADJOINING TEMPLE OF PEACE PROVIDES ROMANS WITH A
SPACE FOR CONTEMPLATION AT THE HEART OF THE CITY.

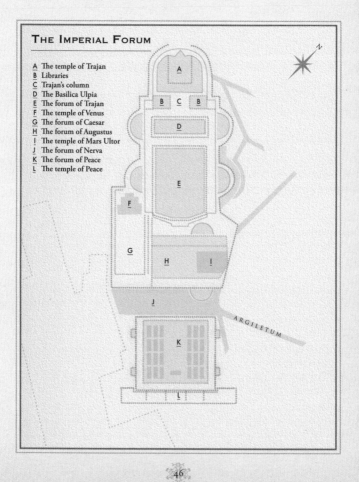

### THE IMPERIAL FORUM

A  The temple of Trajan
B  Libraries
C  Trajan's column
D  The Basilica Ulpia
E  The forum of Trajan
F  The temple of Venus
G  The forum of Caesar
H  The forum of Augustus
I  The temple of Mars Ultor
J  The forum of Nerva
K  The forum of Peace
L  The temple of Peace

ARGILETUM

*The Basilica Ulpia located within the forum of Trajan.*

## THE FORUM OF JULIUS CAESAR

Caesar's forum was rebuilt and the temple of Venus Genetrix was rededicated by the emperor Trajan. Its inspiration came from the squares of the Persians, and it is to this day a place where Romans learn the laws and seek justice. You will find all sorts of art treasures here, including the image of caesar in military dress, exquisite pictures of Ajax and of Medea, and even a statue of Cleopatra. The pearls from Britain are a curiosity, but far better examples can be found in other parts of the empire.

It is also possible to observe the school children at their lessons in the colonnade.

## THE FORUM OF AUGUSTUS

Legal business expanded under Augustus and a new forum was built with its temple of Mars the Avenger (dedicated prior to the Battle of Philippi). The original version took some 40 years to build, and Hadrian has since restored the forum.

What is most remarkable is the statuary, where all the heroes of the republic are represented, molded into an Augustan vision of the past that creates a unity of purpose and conquest. It was from here in the first years of the empire that generals set out for their commands, and it was to this place that the embassies of foreign peoples came.

The statues are compelling, and inscriptions make clear the nature of their subjects' fame. Aeneas, Romulus, Appius Claudius, Scipio Africanus, and of course Augustus are all here. However, there is just one statue of a woman: Cornelia, who wished simply to be known as the mother of her two sons, the Gracchi brothers, rather than as the daughter of the conqueror of Carthage.

## THE FORUM OF NERVA

Constructed within the space between Augustus' forum and Vespasian's temple of Peace, the project was begun by Domitian and completed by Nerva.

It is a narrow but ingenious example of a forum, with a rather exquisite temple dedicated to Minerva. From here, make sure that you find the time to visit the temple of Peace, dedicated in the sixth year of Vespasian's reign. He was responsible for moving Nero's great art collection here from the Golden House, and for setting the statuary in a planted (almost wooded) piazza.

In what was described at the time as one of the noblest structures in the world, you can rest from your tour of the city, and consider the quality of both the ancient and modern sculptures on display. There is also both a map of Rome and a map of the empire, set up under Septimius Severus, inscribed into marble.

## THE FORUM OF TRAJAN

The largest and the last forum to be constructed by an emperor, Trajan's forum eclipses all others both in area and the volume of its basilica.

The column, surmounted by an image of Trajan and decorated with carved scenes of the conquest of Dacia, is an object of curiosity in its own right. Visitors can ascend the stairs built inside it and look out onto the great fora of Rome's emperors and wonder at the power of this people, who rule over so much of the world.

The libraries at the base of the column contain a wonderful collection of works in both Latin and Greek. There is also the adjacent temple dedicated to Trajan, as well as the markets close at hand, arranged over several different levels.

## THE CAPITOLINE HILL

Passing through the Arch of Septimius Severus, you will see a space surrounded by temples dedicated to Saturn, Concordia, Vespasian, and Titus.

The treasury of Rome is housed within the temple of Saturn, where young senators attached to the mint discuss the images to be used on Rome's coins. It is also from here that matters relating to the customs duties paid—for example, in the provinces—are administered. In fact, all across the forum you will see small offices

*Trajan's column features a frieze depicting his military campaign against the Dacians.*

in which scribes and attendants to the magistrates of Rome are dealing with the affairs of the state.

A visit to the temple of Concordia should not be missed, particularly as this was the first temple to be constructed to a plan that allowed natural light in through a series of windows, so that Tiberius' impressive collection of statues might be better displayed to the people.

Moving on, the temple of Vespasian and Titus (restored by Septimius Severus) features statues of these two likeable emperors. Vespasian's eyes and features reflect what is generally accepted to be a quiet amusement at the world around him; a view of life confirmed when prior to his death he said: "Oh dear, I think I am becoming a god."

Immediately behind the temples lies the Tabularium—the record office of Rome. Here you will find

*The temple of Jupiter Optimus Maximus.*

copies of legal documents and state archives—everything from the discharge of an auxiliary soldier through to the edicts of divine emperors. From here, take the street called Clivus Capitolinus, leading to the temple of Jupiter Optimus Maximus—note on the climb the pit into which the refuse from the temple of Venus is deposited.

## THE TEMPLE OF JUPITER

Nothing can prepare the visitor for the sight of the temple of Jupiter on the Capitoline Hill. It excels all else in Rome and is recognized by all as being the temple from which Rome's eternity springs.

The temple is a spacious structure that contains numerous works of art, the quality of which is remarkable, causing some visitors to leave the temple with a feeling that the statues sometimes come to life and breathe. Indeed, there is nothing in the inhabited world that is more magnificent than this glorious edifice; even the temple of Serapis in Alexandria, though taller, fails to come close. It is difficult to find the words to do this mighty structure justice. It dominates the Roman skyline, and its glittering golden roof with its gilded statues can be seen from as far away as Tibur and Praeneste—it really is one of the essential sites to take in during any trip to Rome.

The temple was struck by lightning 15 times during the

## TRAFFIC ACCIDENTS

Beware of wheeled traffic on the streets leading up hills. Clivus Capitolinus is one such street that has been associated with some severe injuries, and even deaths, when wagons have run out of control. The problem often occurs when mules pulling wagons are overloaded or have to stop halfway up the hill due to congestion.

Should you be unlucky enough to be involved in an accident, it is worth noting that you can sue not just the owner of the wagon that hit you, but also the person or persons responsible for that wagon stopping (often the cause is a spilled load from another wagon).

reigns of Septimius Severus and Caracalla—an omen that all would not be well for Rome—but today any damage that was done has been repaired.

# THE PALATINE HILL AND THE EMPEROR'S PALACE

AT THE VERY CENTER OF THE CITY LIES THE PALATINE: THE LOCATION OF THE ORIGINAL CITY. ONLY THE EXTREMELY WEALTHY LIVED HERE DURING THE REPUBLIC, AND NOW THE EMPERORS HAVE CREATED THEIR GREAT PALACE, WHICH INDEED TAKES ITS NAME FROM THE WORD PALATINE.

## THE IMPERIAL PALACE

Ask your litter bearers to drop you off at the Porta Mugonia, close to the Arch of Titus on the Via Sacra. From here, walk up the paved road that leads to the forum of the Palatine. It is possible, by special arrangement with the prefect of the Praetorian Guard, to take a tour of the palace.

Today you can see the original houses of Augustus and Livia. The modesty of their lifestyle speaks volumes. How did such a modest man hold sway over the Roman world for more than 50 years?

Those wanting to see Roman architecture at its finest should move on to the vast chambers built by Rabirius for the emperor Domitian. He also extended the Aqua Claudia to the Palatine and brought aqueduct water into the palace. Septimius Severus was responsible for building the artificial terraces that lead out from

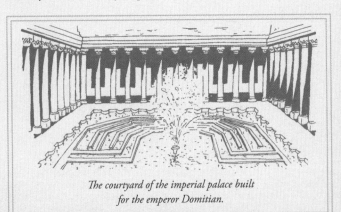

*The courtyard of the imperial palace built for the emperor Domitian.*

WHAT TO EXPECT

# THE TAUROBOLIUM

The priests of Cybele can arrange this rite of purification and rebirth, in which you stand in a pit with a grating over it. A bull is led to stand on the grating directly above your head. It is then slaughtered, drenching you in its blood.

the Palatine toward the Circus Maximus. On these structures, he had the baths and a new imperial box built—allowing the imperial family to watch the events in the circus without the inconvenience of having to leave the palace.

Now the efforts of the emperors are consumed by military affairs in the provinces, and the palace is just a reminder that this was once where matters of life and death for so many were decided.

## OTHER PLACES OF INTEREST

After viewing the palace, proceed to the western limit of the hill close to the Scalae Caci. Here you will find the hut of Romulus (there is a second one on the Capitoline Hill).

The Romans have rebuilt this relic whenever it has been destroyed by fire, and it remains a link with the city's foundation.

Close at hand are the temple of Victory and the temple of Magna Mater or Cybele.

The defeats inflicted by Hannibal on Rome in the Second Punic War resulted in a crisis of confidence. As a consequence, the Sibylline Books (that record the sayings of the Sibyl at Cumae) were consulted, and it was decreed that the Black Stone sacred to Magna Mater should be brought to Rome. With it came a group of Phrygian priests, who organize worship. Like the consort of the goddess, these priests are castrated; they do this themselves on initiation.

From here, descend to the Lupercal, not the original cave where the wolf nurtured the infants Romulus and Remus, but in fact a grotto constructed by the emperor Augustus. Whatever its origins, it is from here that the *Luperci* priests purify the city on the day of the *Lupercalia*.

# FROM THE COLOSSEUM TO THE CIRCUS MAXIMUS

STARING UP AT THE COLOSSEUM, OR FLAVIAN AMPHITHEATER, ONE WONDERS WHETHER THE HUMAN EYE CAN ACTUALLY SEE THE TOP OF THE BUILDING. HOW APPROPRIATE THAT A BUILDING FOR THE ENTERTAINMENT OF THE PEOPLE SHOULD BE BUILT OVER THE PALACE OF THE HATED TYRANT NERO.

### THE COLOSSEUM

When Vespasian came to power, he began an ambitious new project: the largest amphitheater in the world. For a long time the Romans had been dissatisfied with the stone amphitheater that was built by Statilius Taurus during the age of Augustus, and Vespasian saw an opportunity for a bold statement that would distance his reign from that of Nero.

The tyrant's Golden House was destroyed and, using the slave laborers from the Jewish Revolt, the Colosseum was built in its place. It was completed after Vespasian's death, and its opening was celebrated with a flurry of famous spectacles that emperors to this day seek to emulate. It has stood here and been the site for the most lavish forms of beast hunting for 220 years, but it should be noted that there has been much restoration work over that time to maintain it and to recover its

splendor following fire damage. The most recent restoration was made by Alexander Severus and was funded by the tax imposed on male and female prostitutes in the city.

Standing before the Flavian Amphitheater is the Colossus commissioned by Nero, a bronze statue of the Sun God. The work is by Zenodorus, and it must be the largest statue of its kind in the whole world. The Colosseum's proportions are vast: with 80 entrances, it can comfortably seat 50,000 spectators.

The atmosphere at events here is incredible: the roar of the crowd and the quality of the entertainment are sure to convert anyone to Rome's great addictions: beast fights and gladiators.

It is possible to take a tour of the labyrinthine corridors that lie below the arena floor, and to see all the winching devices that deliver animals and fighters into the

arena. This advanced technology is what makes the games here so spectacular, as it turns the choreography of violence and death into an art form.

### THE CIRCUS MAXIMUS

Leaving the Colosseum, follow the road along what is the valley between the Palatine and Caelian Hills, and before long you will arrive at the Circus Maximus, a structure capable of seating 250,000 spectators. It is a sacred structure—the central barrier holds numerous holy items—and its divine conception underpins the entire edifice. Twelve starting gates represent the twelve months of the year and the twelve signs of the zodiac. The chariots have four horses, matching the four seasons of the year, and there are also four teams: the reds, blues, greens, and whites. Finally, the seven laps represent the seven planets.

The circus and the shows it holds are in harmony with the divine order and honor the gods. No wonder they are so popular with those who are said to rule over an empire without end.

*The thrill of chariot racing in the Circus Maximus.*

# THE CAMPUS MARTIUS

THE FIELD ON WHICH YOUNG MEN LEARNED THE ART OF
WAR IN THE REPUBLIC BECAME A CENTER FOR RECREATION
UNDER THE EARLY EMPERORS. TODAY YOU WILL FIND A
MIXTURE OF PARKLAND AND NOTABLE MONUMENTS.

Ask your litter bearers to drop you off near the Mulvian Bridge, and from this rather insalubrious part of town take a boat down the Tiber to the mausoleum of Augustus.

Your boat-trip will help you place the landmarks of the city in context—the temples on the hills, and then before you the mausoleum: the burial place of the first emperors topped off with its gleaming statue of Augustus. Note, as you alight, the more recent mausoleum built by Hadrian on the far bank of the Tiber. In front of the mausoleum of Augustus, are the twin columns on which are inscribed his own accounts of his achievements.

From here, cross the massive pavement of the sundial—the pointer or gnomon is an obelisk, and visit the altar of Augustan Peace located at the very edge of the sacred boundary or *pomerium* within which weapons were traditionally not carried. The friezes show all the members of the Augustan family and many noble senators. It is a vision of the Augustan world as a partnership between an emperor and the senate, whereas today the chief partners of state are the emperors and the army.

Go down the Via Lata, through the Arch of Claudius, which celebrates his victory over the Britons, and the new arch under construction for Diocletian's forthcoming visit. Other victory monuments on this road include the column of Marcus Aurelius, which is well worth climbing to see the view west across the Campus Martius and the river to the Janiculum, south to the Capitoline Hill, and east to the Esquiline.

## THE PANTHEON

Turn right and enter the main area of monuments. Many of these were the work of Marcus Agrippa, the right-hand man of Augustus. His baths and *stagnum* (formal lake) lie at the very center of the Campus.

Next to the baths is the Pantheon. The monument seen today is a reconstruction ordered by Hadrian, and further restoration was completed under Septimius Severus. The approach to the temple does not give any hint of the circular interior that supports the largest dome in the world. The interior space of the temple takes on the role of a forum; and it was here that Hadrian held his meetings with the senate. All the gods are represented within this triumph of Roman engineering. The entire space is lit by a window in the roof. The play of light at different times of the day is fascinating, and it is worth revisiting several times during your stay.

## BEYOND THE PANTHEON

The vast *saepta* or voting hall is adjacent to the Pantheon. Completed by Agrippa, it was designed for the holding of popular elections (abolished in the first year of the reign of Tiberius), but has been used by the emperors to display wonders such as unfamiliar animals, including hippopotami and rhinoceroses, or even stranger items such as the remains of a centaur: half-man, half-horse.

Passing the baths of Agrippa and the stagnum, from where there are views across the water to the baths of Nero (rebuilt by Alexander Severus and now known as the Thermae Alexandrinae), you will arrive at the Odeon and Stadium built by the emperor Domitian. The former houses musical competitions in a covered theater holding 11,000, while the latter is home to Greek-style athletics watched by as many as 30,000. The supporting arches of

*The Pantheon boasts the world's largest dome.*

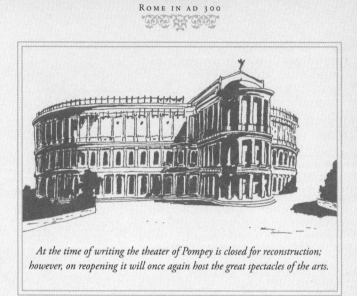

*At the time of writing the theater of Pompey is closed for reconstruction; however, on reopening it will once again host the great spectacles of the arts.*

the Stadium are populated by male and female prostitutes, presumably meeting the demand created by the steamy atmosphere within the adjacent baths of Nero.

From here, take the Via Recta to Nero's bridge over the Tiber. Here, you can see the great mausoleum of Hadrian to the north, while to the south steam emerges from the fissure in the ground at the place known as the Tarentum (an entrance to the underworld, or at least so some say). Follow one of the streets running parallel to the river past the Trigarium—which contains a training track for young would-be charioteers where instruction can be provided—and through the densely inhabited area close to the river. Further down the

street, turn left and you will arrive at the theater of Pompey. This was the first theater to be constructed in stone in the city, topped off with a temple of Victory. It is a copy of the theater found in the city of Mytilene, in Asia Minor. It has been restored on numerous occasions and is currently closed once again to allow restoration work to continue undisturbed.

Moving east, visitors will pass a set of early temples, prior to reaching the theater of Balbus, smaller than that of Pompey, but constructed in the Augustan age to a very similar plan and alignment. You may wish to visit the collection of antique statues in the Porticus Octaviae and also the Circus Flaminius.

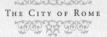
## THE FORUM BOARIUM

Leaving the Campus Martius, enter the area that is known as the forum Boarium. Make toward the theater of Marcellus that dominates the skyline, and takes its name from Augustus' nephew. It was one of the places where Septimius Severus celebrated the inauguration of the new age of 110 years at his Ludi Saeculares. The theater itself was subsequently restored by Alexander Severus and performances are staged here today in front of huge audiences of 20,000 or more.

Visitors may wish to linger among the temples dating back to republican times, before taking the bridge of Fabricius to Tiber island.

The island itself is shaped and embellished to appear like a vast ship anchored in the middle of the river. There are good views of other bridges and the ancient river port.

If you have time, make your way downstream to the Pons Sublicius, Rome's first bridge, which is still built from wood.

## HORATIUS AT THE BRIDGE

It was at an earlier incarnation of the Pons Sublicius that in early times Horatius Cocles, with his companions Spurius Lartius and Titus Herminius, held off an entire Etruscan army. His compatriots cut down the bridge behind him, thwarting Rome's would-be invaders. Horatius then leapt into the raging Tiber, but whether he made it safely to the other side is the subject of much debate.

# AUTHENTIC ROME: THE SUBURA

MANY VISITORS AVOID THIS AREA, BUT IT IS THE HEART
OF ROME AND IT IS HERE THAT YOU WILL SEE THE
INHABITANTS AT WORK AND AT PLAY——AND THERE ARE
AMPLE OPPORTUNITIES TO OBSERVE BOTH.

Immediately to the rear of the forum of Augustus and the other imperial fora lies the Subura: a low-lying district filling the valleys between the Viminal, Quirinal, and Esquiline hills and extending up onto the lower reaches of the hills via the Clivus Suburbanus.

This is the most densely populated part of the city and some notable figures hale from here, Julius Caesar among them. Although often described as dirty, wet, stuffy, and noisy, this is where you will get the best view of daily life in Rome, and the splendid monuments of the city center seem to be a world away.

Few children, regardless of sex, venture here without a chaperone; whereas it is the destination of every young man, after he has swapped the trappings of childish dress for the toga of adulthood. There is much to see and to be experienced here, and the area is famous for its barbers' shops and prostitutes. Also, the prices of goods seem to be somewhat cheaper than in the more famous streets of the city, such as the Argiletum.

The Subura's reputation for violence is not unjustified and it

## THE PLEBS AND THE EMPERORS TODAY

You will find among the people of Rome some discontent with the new government. For the first time in 450 years, taxation is planned to be imposed upon all Rome's inhabitants, while threats of disruption to the supply of imported food from Africa have also led to rioting in the city. Moves have also been made by the emperors to reduce the number of the Praetorian Guard, on the reasonable grounds that the emperors are seldom resident in Rome. Those soldiers who have been laid off harbor some strong feelings, but are unlikely to take action without a leader.

*The porticus of Livia is one of the most
relaxing places to visit in the city of Rome.*

is unwise to linger here after dark, although many good fighters have enjoyed the challenge.

### THE PORTICUS OF LIVIA

Whatever the reputation of the region, most visitors travel along the Clivus Suburbanus to view the porticus of Livia (the wife of Augustus). The site was bequeathed to Augustus by Vedius Pollio—one of the richest freed slaves of the time, who infamously fed clumsy slaves to his lampreys.

Pollio's house was the epitome of luxury and not to the emperor's taste. He demolished the structure, and on the site Livia built the beautiful porticus that bears her name, although it is actually dedicated to Concordia.

After passing the fountains on the Clivus Suburbanus, you will come to the monumental steps that lead into the porticus. The transition from the street is dramatic: you enter a garden that is exquisitely arranged and is adorned with a collection of paintings. Leaving the porticus at the opposite side from which you entered, turn left to approach the baths of Trajan—a much larger structure stretching out across the Oppian Peak (seepp.69).

# THE NORTH AND EAST OF THE CITY

ON THE HILLS OVERLOOKING THE SUBURA AND THE CAMPUS MARTIUS YOU WILL FIND THE CONTRAST OF DENSELY OCCUPIED STREETS, BUT ALSO GARDENS TO RELAX IN. HERE ARE SOME OF THE MOST BEAUTIFUL PARKLANDS, FROM WHICH YOU WILL GAIN VIEWS RIGHT ACROSS ROME AND BE ABLE TO PICK OUT THE GREAT MARVELS OF THE CITY.

### THE GARDENS OF ROME

The Romans have developed a form of landscape architecture that draws its inspiration from the countryside (*rus*) and the technology of the architecture found in the city. There are buildings, vistas, landscaped hills, valleys, and rivers, all dotted with sculpture and a wide range of plants imported from all over the empire. There is little that is rustic about, for example, the auditorium of Maecenas, apart from the vegetation that is incorporated into its wall decoration.

The gardens of Lucullus are as famous for their sense of luxury as their owner was, when he skulked here while Pompey and Caesar held sway. The gardens of Sallust have

## THE VILLA OF MAXENTIUS

You may wish to take the Via Labicana from the Porta Labicana on the Esquiline for about six miles. Here you will find the private estate of Maxentius who, because of the workings of the Tetrarchy, is not in line to succeed his father Maximian. However, current rumors of a coup backed by the Praetorian Guard persist, and Maxentius does little to dampen speculation, welcoming most visitors, and seeking to curry favor with those of influence.

been the residence in the city of numerous emperors—including Vespasian, who found the palace of Nero a little grand for his tastes. It was in the gardens of Licinianus that the emperor Gallienus planned to set up a colossal statue of himself to look upon Rome from the Esquiline Hill.

Here you will find temples, colonnades, and all the architecture that you might associate with Rome, but in a rural setting. All the gardens open to the public are worth a visit, but it is suggested that visitors go to the gardens of Lucullus and the gardens of Sallust, and then the baths of Diocletian and the camp of the Praetorian Guard. It is also possible to view the walls built by Aurelian, and to see where the wall has been built over or against apartment blocks.

## THE BATHS OF DIOCLETIAN

The building site that will become the baths of Diocletian covers a vast area, the size of a provincial city. Work was begun two years ago on Maximian's return from Africa. When completed—in five years' time—these baths will exceed all the previous *thermae* (hot baths) of Rome. When fully functional, the baths will be supplied with aqueduct water taken from the Aqua Marcia.

Visitors may view the building site and see how the Romans employ the skills and management techniques that enable larger projects than those undertaken in the past.

## THE CAMP OF THE PRAETORIAN GUARD

The emperor Augustus' bodyguard, which was to become the Praetorians, was originally billeted around the city, and it was only under Tiberius that they gained what was then the first army camp with walls made of concrete conglomerate and faced with bricks.

The permanent camp gave this force of soldiers greater coherence and the ability to make or break emperors. The protectors of the emperor could all too easily become his murderers: the first to be murdered was Caligula, and the first to be made emperor by them was Claudius.

The loyalty of the Praetorians to the current regime is a source of continual speculation, and rumors abound that they may attempt to place Maxentius, the biological son of Maximian, on the throne.

It is sometimes possible to gain admission and to see the numerous altars set up by the soldiers to the gods.

*The camp of the Praetorian Guard on a coin issued during the reign of Claudius.*

# THE SOUTH OF THE CITY

THE SOUTH OF THE CITY DESERVES A VISIT. DOMINATED BY THE AVENTINE AND CAELIAN HILLS, IT WILL HELP THE VISITOR TO APPRECIATE THE FULL VARIETY OF SIGHTS THAT MAKE UP THE ETERNAL CITY OF ROME.

### THE AVENTINE

The Aventine Hill has always deferred to the Palatine. In fact it was on the Aventine that Remus saw more birds in his competition with Romulus, who was stationed on the Palatine, to decide the founding place of Rome (although the latter cheated); and it was here that the plebs met to frustrate their enslavement by the patricians in republican times.

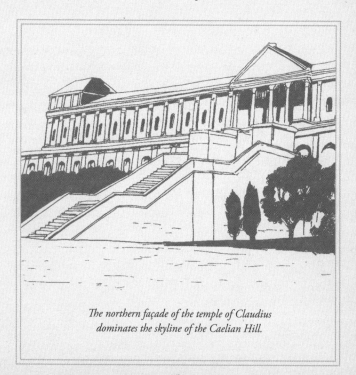

*The northern façade of the temple of Claudius dominates the skyline of the Caelian Hill.*

Today, there are numerous lavish houses here. Visitors should make for the temple of Diana that is sacred not just to Rome, but also to her Latin allies. There are numerous other ancient temples here—many to gods whom the Romans relocated from the cities of their enemies, via the rite of *evocatio*; for example, the Volsinii lost their god Vortumnus, and with him any divine aid in their struggle with Rome.

In more recent times, a sanctuary of the Syrian deity Jupiter Dolichenus has been set up, as well as a temple to Isis. The baths of Decius and baths of Antonianus are also worth a visit.

### THE CAELIAN

Descending from the Aventine cross the valley over to the Caelian Hill. The major monument to see is the rusticated temple of Claudius, which was completed by the emperor Vespasian and continues to dominate the skyline. However, there are more recent developments on the Caelian, not least the building of the Castra Peregrina—a massive transit camp for soldiers and new recruits—as well as the Castra Equitum Singularium, for cavalry soldiers resident in Rome (a thousand in total). You will see many provincial soldiers here, especially Germans and Pannonians.

Crossing the Caelian Hill, drop down to the beginning of the Via Appia and continue to the recently constructed walls of Aurelian. These walls surround the city that may now be described as being shaped like a seven-pointed star. These are the most-up-to-date and most extensive defenses that can be seen anywhere today. Return toward the center of the city and visit the baths of Caracalla.

### THE BATHS OF CARACALLA

The baths of Caracalla are the largest functioning thermae in the city. They contain not just the bath building itself, but also two libraries, a running track, and an exercise area.

The interior of the baths does not disappoint, with glass mosaics, abundant fountains, vistas from the male to female bathing areas and vice-versa; but maybe the greatest sight is the hot room or *cella solearis*, with a vaulted ceiling so high that it would seem impossible to construct anything to rival this marvel of human design.

There is another side to the baths, only seen by those who work there. If you ask for either Cucumius or Victoria and pay enough, they will arrange for you to see the workers' view of the structure. There is a paved road running below, and a series of labyrinthine corridors to enable the attendants to travel unseen. There is even a sizeable shrine set up to the invincible sun god Mithras.

# THE RIVER PORT, TRASTEVERE, AND THE JANICULUM

THE RIVER TIBER GAVE THE CITY OF ROME ITS LIFE MORE THAN A THOUSAND YEARS AGO. TODAY IT LIES AT THE HEART OF THE SUPPLY SYSTEM OF THIS MEGA-CITY, BRINGING IN GOODS FROM RIGHT ACROSS THE EMPIRE. NO DOUBT THE RIVER, AS MUCH AS JUPITER, WILL GUARANTEE THE CITY'S SURVIVAL IN THE FUTURE.

## THE TIBER

The Tiber in flood brought the infants Romulus and Remus to the Lupercal, at the base of the Palatine Hill. The Romans believe that their rivers are gods, and Tiber seems to be one of the unruly ones. It often floods the city and each inundation is regarded as a portent of danger. Julius Caesar considered cutting a new course for the Tiber to the west of the Janiculum, as a means to prevent flooding in the city.

The banks of the river are maintained by curators, and in recent years, under Diocletian's guidance, they have been most diligent in establishing what is public property on the banks of the Tiber. All along the river there are numerous warehouses (*horrea*) and places for boats to offload their cargoes to be distributed throughout the city on the backs of donkeys. The scale of importation can be seen in the mound of pottery that continues to grow to the south of the river port: amphorae are taken here and deliberately smashed to create a hill made out of the containers within which olive oil is transported to Rome.

## TRASTEVERE OR TRANSTIBERIM

The XIVth region of Rome lies across the river. Six bridges link the region to the city center, and it is now defended by the walls built under the emperor Aurelian. This is also where the Via Aurelia and the road from Portus (the port of Rome) enter the city. What you will find here is a congested region that is as much part of the city as the Subura.

Well worth a visit is the *naumachia* of Augustus—a lake constructed for the display of naval fights and the hunting of animals in water. If a performance is on when you are in Rome, go and see

the mythological re-enactments: criminals decked out as Leander to be drowned in the waves, and sea battles from Greek history. The synchronized swimming of naked sea nymphs is also popular (see pp.106–7).

### THE JANICULUM

Only recently recognized as a hill of Rome, the Janiculum takes its name from a village that was originally the site of a Roman fort or outpost, to observe any approach by the Etruscans. (Even in the time of caesar a permanent signal post was maintained here.)

Today the Janiculum is famous for its sanctuary of the Syrian god Jupiter Heliopolitanus, just outside the city walls, and you will see many visitors from Syria and the east at the sanctuary.

*A tempestuous figure, responsible for the many floods of the city, the river god Tiber nevertheless aided in Rome's foundation.*

# THE MUST-VISIT BATHS OF ROME

PERHAPS IT IS IMPOSSIBLE TO SEE ALL OF ROME—THERE ARE AFTER ALL SO MANY HILLS, SO VAST AN AREA, SO MANY STREETS, AND SO MANY TEMPLES. INVARIABLY THIS WILL TAKE ITS TOLL ON THE WEARY VISITOR, SO WHY NOT RELAX AND SOAK UP SOME OF THE UNIQUE ATMOSPHERE AT SOME OF ROME'S MANY BATHS?

It is well worth spending rather longer at the baths than just the hour or so that it takes to enjoy the cold, warm, and hot rooms. Many larger baths have been built over the last century, and it seems that emperors are simply not taken seriously unless they manage to provide the people of Rome with a new bathing experience. The following baths are well worth a visit.

**The baths of Agrippa**—the first monumental set of baths established in the city. The structure was rebuilt by Hadrian, but still contains pictures of Ajax and Aphrodite from Cyzicus, and also the giant lion that originally stood in the entrance hall.

**The baths of Aurelian**—a recent addition, to be found in Rome's XIVth region across the Tiber. They were designed to give the best possible bathing experience in the winter months.

**The baths of Caracalla**—built by Caracalla, but restored by the emperor Aurelian some 30 years ago. The terraces upstairs (cella solearis) permit views of the exercises performed in the palaestras, an intriguing view of the various regimen and fitness activities undertaken at the baths.

> ## OTHER SITES NOT TO BE MISSED
>
> ❖ Temple of Jupiter on the Capitoline
> ❖ Temple of Venus and Rome (currently closed for restoration)
> ❖ Pantheon
> ❖ Forum Romanum—old forum
> ❖ Temple of Peace
> ❖ Forum of Trajan
> ❖ Theater of Pompey
> ❖ Odeon
> ❖ Stadium
> ❖ Colosseum

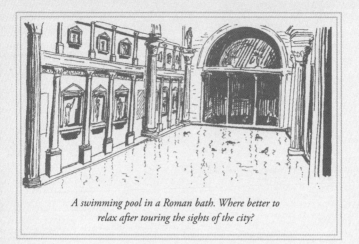

*A swimming pool in a Roman bath. Where better to relax after touring the sights of the city?*

**The baths of Decius**—built by Trajan Decius 50 years ago on the Aventine Hill close to the temple of Diana: about an eighth of the size of the baths of Caracalla, but an interesting design that appears to be based on the baths found in the African provinces.

**The baths of Diocletian**—though still under construction, this site is worth a visit as when the baths are eventually completed they are promised to be the most magnificent in the city, and an important addition for those staying on or near the Quirinal Hill.

**The baths of Nero**—known today as the baths of Alexander Severus after the extensive rebuild and expansion of the original baths of Nero. Now, 70 years since it was rebuilt, it still contains the level of luxury offered by Nero's original baths.

**The baths of Sura**—constructed by L. Licinius Sura, a supporter of the emperor Trajan, in the XIIIth region of the city, on the Aventine Hill, and restored by the emperor Gordian. It contains a famous gymnasium.

**The baths of Titus**—built by Titus and opened to coincide with the dedication of the Colosseum. The baths were extensively restored 60 years ago, and are one of the smaller of the imperial thermae.

**The baths of Trajan**—designed by Apollodorus of Damascus and opened by the emperor Trajan on the Oppian Hill. Within the substructures of the platform on which the baths are built, you can still visit some surviving remains of Nero's Golden House.

# SURROUNDING
# AREAS

*Given the chance, visitors should try to venture
further afield than Rome itself, especially to see the
cities that were once Rome's rivals. Also, all should
consider a trip to the coast, and where better to go than
the Bay of Naples with all its history and culture and
some pleasures that you will not find even in Rome?*

*Today power has shifted away from Rome and can
only be seen in action in the emperor's court in
Mediolanum (Milan) or in the other cities of northern
Italy—to reflect these changed circumstances, a trip
north is also included here.*

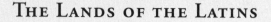

# THE LANDS OF THE LATINS

ROME DID NOT ALWAYS RULE SUPREME; THE CITIES OF THE
LATINS, SOME LESS THAN 20 MILES AWAY, WERE ONCE HER
RIVALS FOR POWER. NOT TO BE MISSED ARE THE NEARBY
CITIES OF PRAENESTE AND TIBUR. THESE TWO, BOTH JUST A
SHORT TRIP FROM THE CITY, PROVIDE AMPLE OPPORTUNITY TO
EXAMINE THE ROMAN COUNTRYSIDE FIRST HAND.

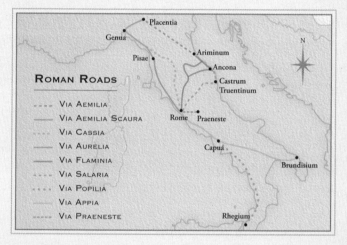

**ROMAN ROADS**

- - - - VIA AEMILIA
────── VIA AEMILIA SCAURA
· · · · · VIA CASSIA
────── VIA AURELIA
────── VIA FLAMINIA
- - - - VIA SALARIA
· · · · · VIA POPILIA
────── VIA APPIA
- - - - - VIA PRAENESTE

### THE ROAD TO PRAENESTE

Leave the city of Rome by the
Porta Praenestina. It is worth,
even if only briefly, examining
the way the walls of Aurelian
have incorporated the aqueducts
entering the city to create a truly
monumental gateway from which
runs the Via Praenestina. The road
is well built and paved with the
hardest black paving stones.

At the third milestone, you may
wish to linger at the villa of the
Gordians (briefly rulers of Rome
some 60 years ago), which features
some 200 imported marble
columns and three basilicas.
Their family tomb resembles the
shape, if not the dimensions, of
the Pantheon. Continue on the
road until you reach the 12th
milestone.

To the left of the road, as you
approach the former city of Gabii,
you will observe a temple within
a wood. It is dedicated to Juno

and has been the site of numerous cures. The temple, wood, and small temple were created here some 500 years ago. The goddess Fortuna is also venerated at altars close to the sanctuary. From here continue on the road for a further 11 miles to Praeneste.

## PRAENESTE AND THE SANCTUARY OF FORTUNA

You will see the sanctuary from quite a distance; it dominates the city, and you might even feel that Fortuna herself is watching your approach. On arrival at the city gates, take the road that leads to the forum. You are advised to spend the night here, rather than hastening back to Rome, and should arrange accommodation.

The sanctuary is approached from the forum via a series of

*The upper terrace of the Sanctuary of Fortuna at Praeneste.*

## THE GODDESS FORTUNA

The Romans believe that the goddess Fortuna can raise a man to prominence, only to dash him down once he has achieved it. She is a fickle deity, as is witnessed by the fortunes of the numerous men who have recently held power over the Roman Empire only to have that power (and their lives) snatched away.

ramps that are designed to conceal and then reveal the *tholos* (circular tomb) of the goddess. You will hear the sound of running water as you make your way up the ramps, until you reach the upper terrace that has been perfectly designed for taking the auspices (reading the will of the gods from the flight of birds). Moving onward, you enter the sacred area, where we are told Numerius Suffustius split the rock from which a set of tablets for divination sprang. At this sacred place, you will see the statue of Fortuna with the infant gods Jupiter and Juno seated in her lap.

Return to Rome, either on the Via Praenestina, or on the paved road that leads south from Praeneste then joins the Via Labicana.

## THE ROAD TO TIBUR

Take the Via Tiburtina from Rome; you will pass through the cemeteries and villas of the famous and then enter a quite different landscape, close to the River Anio. Here you will find the quarries from which travertine is cut with saws; you will already have passed the wagons on the road heading slowly to Rome to supply this prized stone to Maximian's architects.

Tibur (Tivoli) remained an independent city long after others had been incorporated into the Roman state, and its people became citizens only a little under 400 years ago.

Visitors should make for the sanctuary of Hercules, set on an artificial platform under which runs the Via Tiburtina—a toll is extracted on all sheep using the route to Rome, and the proceeds are kept at the sanctuary. The layout of the sanctuary features a wide rectangular enclosure that surrounds a temple, with a small theater sunk into the terrace. One can see the layout, if not the theater, as the inspiration for the forum of Augustus in Rome, sometimes referred to as the sanctuary of Mars, and it makes sense of Augustus' statement that his forum is narrower than he had intended.

This is a sacred place and contains a record of some of the prophesies of the sibyl that form part of the reconstructed Sibylline Books (the originals were lost in a fire on the Capitoline Hill). These books are consulted in times of crisis, but, in spite of the efforts of the emperor Augustus, still contain numerous false statements and interpolations. However, here in Tibur you will be able to see some of the originals.

## THE QUEEN OF TIBUR

Queen Zenobia of Palmyra once wielded power in the East as though her sons were emperors. She was defeated and captured by Aurelian and duly displayed in a triumphal procession loaded with gems and in golden shackles.

The only female ruler over Romans, her life was spared and she lived with her sons in a villa near Tibur in the manner of a Roman matron. She banqueted in the style of a Persian king, she hunted with the eagerness of a Spaniard, she learned Latin and ensured that her sons spoke that language rather than Greek, and had sex with her husband only when she wished to become pregnant. Many call her a modern Cleopatra, and her villa can easily be found: just ask for the place called Zenobia.

# VILLAS FOR HIRE

Around Tibur you will find numerous villas for hire. These are magnificent dwellings that look out over the River Anio and provide a welcome retreat for anyone wishing to have a little respite from the arduous business of sightseeing in Rome. Many come equipped with staff, not to mention a well-stocked library for the consideration of both serious matters and more leisurely study.

This sanctuary has one of the five largest stores of consecrated treasure in Italy; the others can be found in the temple of Jupiter in Rome, and in temples at Antium, Lanuvium, and Nemi.

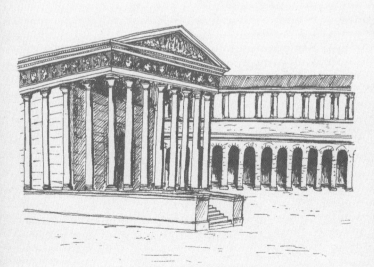

*The sanctuary of Hercules at Tibur, containing one of the largest stores of treasure in all of the Roman world.*

# THE PORT OF ROME

**PORTUS IS AN ENTIRELY ARTIFICIAL HARBOR CONSTRUCTED TO THE NORTH OF THE RIVER TIBER. IT IS NOW ALMOST 360 YEARS OLD, BUT REMAINS A WONDER TO BEHOLD, WITH ITS LIGHTHOUSE AND MASSIVE BREAKWATERS LEADING OUT TO SEA.**

A harbor on the site had been a project of Julius Caesar, but was only realized by the emperor Claudius. The site, two miles north of Ostia, was chosen as it was on marginal land and was ideal for the alleviation of flooding upstream.

The project took over 20 years to complete, and the result was a harbor that was entirely artificial, but not impervious to storm damage. So the emperor Trajan added a new hexagonal inner harbor surrounded by wonderful wharfs and buildings for storage. Previously, grain had been imported to Puteoli on the bay of Naples, from where smaller boats brought it in to Ostia; but today the grain fleet sailing from Egypt and Africa comes straight here to offload its cargo.

Visitors can take either a river boat, if the Tiber is not in spate, or

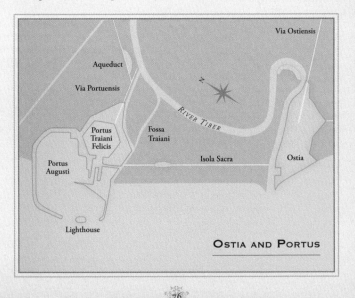

**OSTIA AND PORTUS**

*Portus throngs with the trade of a vast array of goods
being shipped to and from all parts of the empire.*

a carriage by way of the road from Transtiberim (Trastevere). This is a strange city, administratively dependent on Ostia, but in many ways far more important.

You will see vast storage facilities, dedications to the gods and emperors, and the infrastructure of the annona at work, every stage duly checked by state officials engaged in the prevention of fraud. What will strike any observer is that Trajan's hexagonal harbor is a splendid entry point to Rome for those arriving from overseas. What could be more magnificent than first sailing through the Claudian harbor and then entering this basin? On every side is a seemingly unending vision of ships and the transhipment of goods—a revelation of the scale of the business of supplying Rome with food for the plebs and goods to be put on sale in the city.

## THE GREATEST SHIP OF ALL

The largest ship ever to set sail was built from a huge fir tree and was used by Caligula to import the obelisk from Egypt that now stands in the Circus Maximus. The size may today be estimated from the fact that the ship's ballast was made up of 120 bushels of lentils and that the ship was sunk on Claudius' instructions and now forms part of the great mole leading out into the sea.

# OSTIA AND THE COAST

A COLONY OF A FEW HUNDRED WAS FOUNDED 685 YEARS AGO AT OSTIA TO GUARD THE ESTUARY OF THE TIBER. FOR FOUR CENTURIES TRANSHIPMENT OCCURRED JUST OFFSHORE, FROM SEAGOING VESSELS ONTO BARGES TO TAKE THE GOODS UPSTREAM. TODAY, HOWEVER, PRODUCE COMES TO OSTIA VIA PORTUS, CONSTRUCTED TO THE NORTH OF THE TIBER.

## OSTIA

From Portus take one of the many ferryboats down the canal to the River Tiber and on to the river port at Ostia. There is little to delay you here. The city is full of traders doing deals on the price of shipping every possible cargo from every port in the Mediterranean. Much of the city is composed of densely populated apartment blocks, but it has its forum, and the baths of Neptune are impressive—take a look at the double-glazed windows (the use of such advanced technology is not surprising, given that the baths cost more than two million sesterces in the time of Hadrian and Antoninus Pius). There is also a small theater to divert your attention, but perhaps more interesting are the *collegia*

---

WHAT TO EXPECT

## CONTROLLING THE TIBER

Many attempts have been made to restrict the flow of water in the Tiber, but none has really been successful. The canals near Ostia leading to Portus do remove some of the water—but often navigation is hindered by the sheer velocity and quantity of water in the river. However, in summer the upper reaches lack sufficient water for their navigation. Not even the power of modern Rome can control father Tiber, the god that delivered Romulus and Remus to the Lupercal—an action that resulted in the foundation of the city.

(guilds), which act both as dining clubs and as surrogate families—ensuring, for example, that those who die far from home may have a decent burial. Most are organized around a particular trade: *codicarii* (bargemen); *navicularii* (shippers); *fabri* (builders); and so on. If you get a chance, attend a dinner as a guest or simply visit a building owned by the guild that relates most closely to your own profession.

Also worth a visit are the numerous shrines dedicated to the invincible sun god Mithras that are hidden in the apartment blocks—counterintuitively, these recreate a cave and feature a central scene of Mithras slaughtering a bull.

A curious feature of this city is that a number of the streets near the river have been raised, so that today you enter the buildings on what used to be the second story, and the original ground floor has become a basement or simply been abandoned. Unusually, the city of Ostia expanded so rapidly after the harbor at Portus was built that the city wall was demolished in places and the tombs of the dead were removed to allow the city to extend southward.

*The apartment blocks of Ostia, in many of which you will find shrines to Mithras.*

### ALONG THE COAST

There are many villas, some for hire, all down the coast south of Ostia along the Via Severiana. The famous senator Pliny lived here in Trajan's reign. His villa enjoyed views of mountains and of the sea.

The only disadvantage of the villas closer to the Tiber is that they rely on water drawn from wells or collected rainwater rather than aqueducts. There are no towns in this area, but the Vicus Augustanus is a village only in name. Here you will find many of the trappings of urbanism: baths, statues, and a place from which all the villas on the coast are supplied with produce. A little further down the coast is another village, which is supplied with water directly from an aqueduct and so has rather better bathing facilities.

# THE ALBAN HILLS AND THE LAKES SOUTH OF ROME

A SACRED MOUNTAIN UPON WHICH IS SITED THE TEMPLE OF JUPITER LATIARIS (INSET), MOUNT ALBUS OVERLOOKS NOT ONLY ROME, BUT ALSO LAKE ALBANUS—A VAST INLAND LAKE LOCATED IN THE MOUNTAINS.

It was here that Domitian had a palace, and there are many other villas close by on the Via Appia, some even with caves that house statues representing the tangled journey of Odysseus. (The blinding of the Cyclops Polyphemus, and Odysseus' encounter with the sea monster Scylla were once very popular themes for these gigantic sculptures installed in caves adjacent to small dining couches overlooking the lake.)

Septimius Severus set up the Castra Albana to house the troops of the Legio II Parthica. The stone-built camp contains two bath buildings, and there is an amphitheater and a military cemetery outside. Close by is a tunnel built nearly 600 years ago to regulate the level of water on Lake Albanus. The height of the tunnel allows two men to walk the distance from here to the lake.

Above the lake lies the city of Alba Longa, one of the most sacred places for the Latins in Rome's distant past, for it was here that Ascanius, son of Aeneas, founded the dynasty of kings from which Romulus was descended.

## THE SANCTUARY AT NEMUS

From Aricia descend to Lake Nemus (Nemi); here lies the sanctuary of Diana. Numerous sacred springs flow into the lake, including one named after the nymph Egeria, but none flow out.

This is a holy place in a grove of trees. And there is a strange custom, thought to have belonged originally to the Scythians, in which the priest, and king of the wood, has always been a runaway slave. To gain this position the fugitive has slain the previous priest with his own hand; and today you may see a nervous man, armed with a sword, awaiting the day that fate brings him a challenge to his throne and his life.

From the temple, look across the lake that is enclosed by the

ridge of a former volcano: it was here that the emperor Caligula constructed boats as large as palaces for the entertainment of his friends and entourage. Today, these barges lie at the bottom of the lake.

### ALBA FUCENS

There is another town towards the interior named Alba Fucens, lying above Lake Fucinus on the Via Valeria (some 67 miles from Rome). The lake was drained by Claudius, an undertaking as vast as building the harbor at Portus. For Lake Fucinus, we are told, prior to this time filled up with waters from melted snow and created the surrounding marshland.

It was here, in the days of the republic, that Rome's enemies were incarcerated and kept under a careful watch, well away from any of their own people who might visit the capital. Some of these captives died here, and a visitor can see the memorials set up to commemorate these proud men.

*The fabled Lake Nemus, upon which Caligula once hosted lavish parties aboard vast floating barges.*

# ETRURIA

THE ETRUSCANS OR TUSCI HAVE FASCINATED MANY ROMANS, NOT LEAST THE EMPEROR CLAUDIUS (INSET), WHO WROTE AN EXHAUSTIVE HISTORY OF THE PEOPLE FROM WHOM HE DESCENDED. ETRURIA IS FULL OF LAKES AND ROLLING HILLS, IN WHICH THERE ARE NUMEROUS SMALL CITIES. OVERLOOKING THEM ALL IS MOUNT SORACTE IN THE CENTER OF THE TIBER VALLEY.

There is little sign today that Veii had been a powerful rival to Rome, and many places mentioned in Livy's *Ab Urbe Condita* (*From the Foundation of the City*) no longer live up to their historical reputation. There are, however, numerous villas and farms in the region, as well as important quarries and brickyards.

### FROM ROME TO NEPET

Leave Rome, taking the Via Cassia just after the Mulvian bridge, and travel to Baccanas—a place of little interest, so keep going to Sutri. You will see its amphitheater well before you arrive. The walls of the town are more than 800 years old, but provided little protection from the might of Rome two centuries

*The imposing sight of Mount Soracte dominates the Tiber valley.*

## WHAT TO EXPECT

# ETRUSCAN PAPYRUS

Most Romans will tell you that papyrus comes from Egypt; but here in Etruria, on the banks of the lakes, reeds are harvested ready for transport down the Tiber to Rome. There the reed is converted into papyrus and put on sale.

later, when a colony of Latins was forcibly established here. The town chose the wrong side in the war between Octavian and Anthony, and as a consequence land was confiscated and veterans settled, making it one of the most populous towns of the region at the time.

From here take the local road to Nepet, another Etruscan city on which a Latin colony was founded. The local volcanic stone is gray or black and much of the city appears as if in shadow when compared to the golden or rust-colored stone used in other towns.

### ON TO FERONIA

From Nepet take the Via Amerina north. This road in places is only paved to the width of a single carriage, with the other lane composed of gravel. The journey to Falerii Novi takes you directly north in a straight line on bridges over deep valleys and through cuttings filled with antique Etruscan tombs.

The walls and towers of Falerii Novi, a colony founded to ensure the area's loyalty to Rome, are still impressive today. On entering the city, take care driving up the steep hill to the forum. The later amphitheater and theater are also worth a visit, as is the temple on the Arx (the city's highest point).

From the forum turn east and take the road that leads from Falerii Novi to the Via Flaminia, then head south toward Rome. As you pass Mount Soracte, turn off to Feronia on its lower slopes. Here you will find not only a precinct sacred to a local goddess, much venerated both here and in the Sabina, but also the astonishing sight of those possessed by the goddess walking barefoot across red-hot charcoal.

The town was once where the Sabines and Etruscans met to trade and hold festivals—neutral ground, still sacred to both peoples.

# THE SABINA

THE SABINES WERE THE FIRST PEOPLE WITH WHOM THE ROMANS GAINED THE RIGHT OF CONUBIUM (MARRIAGE), AND MANY ROMANS TRACE THEIR ANCESTRY TO THIS REGION. THE EMPEROR VESPASIAN CAME FROM REATE, AND HE, LIKE OTHERS FROM THE SABINA, CONVEYED AN HONESTY SELDOM FOUND IN SENATORS FROM ELSEWHERE. FILLED WITH MOUNTAINS, THE SABINA IS UTTERLY UNLIKE ETRURIA AND PROVIDES A WELCOME CONTRAST TO LIFE IN ROME—RURAL, QUIET, HARD-WORKING, AND HONEST. THE ENTIRE REGION WAS CONQUERED A LITTLE UNDER SIX CENTURIES AGO.

There are few cities in the Sabina, but that is its charm. Amiternum and Reate stand out as the two major cities, while Cures has become more or less a vicus (village), even though the orators in Rome continue to refer to the Romans as Curites (people of Cures). Trebula Mutuesca is, to be honest, also little more than a village, but it was in this tiny place that the emperor Trajan built a sophisticated amphitheater in the hope that it might galvanize a new

*The rural landscapes of the Sabina provide welcome relief for the weary traveler.*

civic tradition. However, it is as though these people simply have no use for the trappings of a city and instead would rather continue producing olive oil, wine, cattle, and the fabulous mules that you see on the roads today.

### FROM ROME TO SABINA

Take the Via Salaria from Rome. One of Italy's most ancient routes, it derives its name from the salt transported from the beds of Ostia to the Sabines. Sheep and cattle were driven down this road to the Forum Boarium (the ancient cattle market) in Rome. It is 48 miles to Reate (Rieti), a distance that can be covered in a single day. Some visitors might like to take the Via Nomentana and visit the town of Nomentum, where the poet Horace had a villa, and from there join the Via Salaria at Eretum. Both roads are well engineered, with excellent viaducts and bridges.

Reate is a land-locked city, but even here, in the temple dedicated to Magna Mater or Cybele, you may still see evidence of the importance of the sea to the empire. No doubt the Sabines have followed Rome's example, where the temple of this goddess is on the Palatine.

To avoid the roads over the high mountains to the west, from Reate take the side road to Interamna Nahars to the north, before moving south along the drove road. This route is often busy, full of animals being led to market in Forum

---

## THE MULES OF THE SABINA

The Sabina is famous for mules bred from male donkeys and female horses, producing a bigger and stronger animal than usual. If you are traveling by carriage then the ones pulling it are most likely from here. Prices vary, but four matching Reate mules have been known to fetch as much as 400,000 sesterces at auction.

*The mules of the Sabina are famed for their strength, and command a high price.*

---

Novum—a town only in name, with its forum and small basilica. Its amphitheater collapsed some time ago, and few people seem to live here, but there are baths fed by an aqueduct, and it is possible to rest at an inn before heading west to the Via Flaminia and returning to Rome.

# THE BAY OF NEAPOLIS AND BACK

NO TRIP TO ROME IS COMPLETE WITHOUT A VISIT TO
CAMPANIA. THE CITIES OF NEAPOLIS, CUMAE, PUTEOLI,
AND CAPUA ARE FAMOUS THROUGHOUT THE WORLD, AS
ARE THE THERMAL BATHS IN THE CITY OF BAIAE. THIS
IS WHERE THE ROMANS HAVE COME TO PLAY FOR ALMOST
FIVE CENTURIES.

### FROM ROME TO CUMAE

This itinerary allows three days to
cover 117 miles, so leave Rome
early by the Via Appia, truly the
"Queen of Roads," built over 600
years ago. As you leave Rome,
notice the impressive arches of
the aqueducts bestriding the
countryside. You will see after
Aricia how the Via Appia runs in
a direct line to Terracina, and you
should be able to travel fast and
reach the Forum Appii by evening.

Once there, take an overnight
barge through the canals
of the marshes and
alight the next
morning at

*Aqueducts march across the landscape
bringing water to Rome.*

Terracina, a city noted for its
harbor and the sanctuary situated
on the hill above the town.

Hasten through Fundi and
Formiae, to Minturnae some 35
miles south, where you should
rest. There are reasonable bathing
facilities, an interesting forum, and
a theater and amphitheater dating
back to the time of Augustus.

The next day, turn off the Via
Appia south of Sinuessa and take
the Via Domitiana down the
coast—the road is a great feat of
engineering built some 200 years
ago. Stop briefly at the bridge over
the River Vulturnus to admire the
triumphal arches built under the
emperor Domitian. You will see
the acropolis of Cumae long before
you reach the city. For advice on
what to do in the Bay of Neapolis
turn to pp.88–91.

### BACK TO ROME

The return journey is more
leisurely, taking in Capua and the
famous cities on the Via Latina.
You will be able to observe the

grids of field boundaries laid out when Rome settled veteran soldiers on the land, destroying all traces of earlier ownership.

From Neapolis, travel 20 miles north to Capua—the city was notable in the past for rivalling the luxuries of Rome. It was here that the gladiators trained, and there is an impressive amphitheater built about 150 years ago. Today, Capua is the capital of the new province of Campania.

From here, travel 15 miles to Teanum Sidicinum, where there are early examples of both a theater and an amphitheater in what was once one of the area's largest cities.

Leaving the city on the Via Latina, you pass through the cities of Venafrum, Casinum, and Aquinum to reach Fabrateria (30 miles). Three miles further on is Fregellae, a city that was destroyed after its rebellion some four centuries ago, and now scarcely more than a village.

Continue north for some 25 miles to Ferentinum, which even today preserves the fabric of an ancient city of the Latins—the walls built with vast irregular blocks with no mortar attest to the advanced technology used here all those years ago.

Rome is a mere 40 miles on from here and you can easily make for the city, but it would be a shame not to turn off the Via Latina and stay overnight at Tusculum in the Alban Hills, enjoying the impressive views down to Rome.

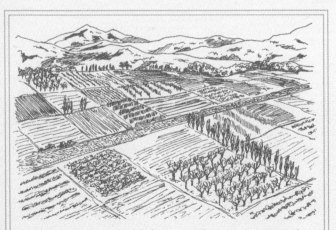

*The Via Appia runs through the Pontine Plain: irrigation has made this area fertile and abundant with produce that is destined for Rome.*

# THE BAY OF NEAPOLIS

FOR NEARLY FIVE CENTURIES, ROMANS HAVE RETREATED TO THEIR VILLAS ON THE BAY OF NEAPOLIS. THE GREEKS SETTLED IN COLONIES HERE A MILLENNIUM AGO. THERE IS PLENTY OF HISTORY—AENEAS EVEN ENTERED THE UNDERWORLD HERE, HAVING CONSULTED THE SIBYL OF APOLLO AS TO WHAT THE FUTURE HELD. THIS IS A LANDSCAPE OF GHOSTLY LAKES, BURIED CITIES, AND BURNT-OUT VOLCANOES—VESUVIUS (INSET) TOWERS ABOVE ALL AND CONTINUES TO BELCH FORTH FUMES AND DEBRIS.

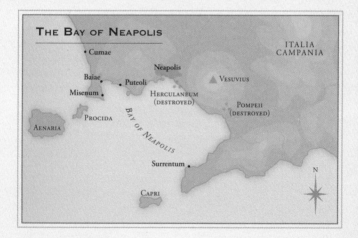

THE BAY OF NEAPOLIS

ITALIA
CAMPANIA

• Cumae

Neapolis

Baiae• •Puteoli

VESUVIUS

Misenum•

HERCULANEUM
(DESTROYED)

POMPEII
(DESTROYED)

PROCIDA

BAY OF NEAPOLIS

AENARIA

Surrentum•

N

CAPRI

## CUMAE

Originally a Greek colony, this city is today a Latin-speaking one. You should enter Cumae through the arch of Domitian and head to the forum, from where you can climb to the acropolis with its splendid views to the north—notice the scars in the landscape where Nero attempted to connect Puteoli to Rome with a canal.

All who visit Rome have heard of the Sibylline Books—the most sacred texts, which the Romans consult in a crisis—but few realize that at Cumae you can descend into the cave of the sibyl, the most sacred priest of Apollo.

From Cumae take the tunnel to Lake Avernus. Although it is enclosed by hills, you can sail into the lake, and it is not hard to imagine that this stretch of water may in fact be connected to the River Styx and the underworld. This impression is enhanced by the fact that no one has ever managed to dive to the bottom of the lake, and many maintain that no bird can fly over it.

## BAIAE

Much is made of the pleasures of Baiae, and some visitors expect unruly parties on the beach and encounters with women as wild as the famous nymphomaniacs of Roman history. In reality, however, most people come to Baiae seeking cures. The first Roman to come was the consul Gnaeus Cornelius, when suffering from arthritis 477 years ago.

Steam rises from the ground and is confined within the bathhouse, producing a far more satisfactory heating of the body than can be found in baths fueled by wood or charcoal. Perhaps this is the reason that Baiae has such a reputation for drunken fornication, as the visitors and their libidos are heated up within this steamy atmosphere.

There are many different baths here, with a vast variety of waters— some attract the sick, others attract pleasure-seekers. Nero did much to develop the resort, but failed in his attempts to divert all the thermal springs into an immense heated swimming pool. Later Domitian linked several pools for the breeding of exotic fish. More recently, the emperor Alexander Severus built new bathhouses in honor of his mother. It was at Baiae that the

*The River Styx separates the living from the souls of the dead.*

## VESUVIUS AND POMPEII

In the reign of Titus, Mount Vesuvius erupted with such force that the towns of Herculaneum and Pompeii were destroyed and remain buried to this day. The more nervous visitor may be reassured to learn that it is nearly a hundred years since Vesuvius' last eruption.

emperor Hadrian died, no doubt taking the waters and hoping for a remedy for his ills.

### MISENUM

Misenum, like Portus, has an inner harbor formed from a lake and connected to the outer harbor by a canal. This is the headquarters of the Roman navy, with its sailors recruited from all the seafaring people of the Mediterranean. You can see the evidence of this in the panoply of names recorded in the cemeteries outside the city.

### PUTEOLI

Originally the Greek colony of Dicearchia and more than a millennium in age, the town of Puteoli was reinvigorated three centuries later when Rome established a colony here. As the empire expanded it grew

to become the port of Rome; however, it lost status once Portus was constructed on the Tiber.

The harbor is remarkable, built from the most durable concrete using the local volcanic sand known as *pozzolana* (which is exported around the Mediterranean).

Unlike other cities, there are not one but two amphitheaters—the most impressive is the third largest in Italy, after the Colosseum of Rome and the later amphitheater built at Capua. Overlooking the harbor and lower city is the acropolis on which Augustus' architect L. Cocceius designed and constructed a temple to his deified emperor.

### NEAPOLIS

Neapolis (Naples) is an old Greek colony and the one city that has managed to preserve some of its Greek heritage with *gymnasia*, *ephebeia* (for the training of youths), and a system of *phratriae* (districts).

It was in the theater at Neapolis that Nero first performed to rapturous applause, while the future emperor Vespasian sat in the audience asleep. The layout of the town is a grid of *plateiai* (wide streets) and *stenopoi* (alleyways)—how the urban planner Hippodamus of Miletus would have set out a city. Many apparently Greek edifices were in fact built by Roman emperors, Augustus' gymnasium among them, and also the theater, at which musical contests are held every five years.

Roman culture has still made its mark in the form of the amphitheater outside the walls of the Greek city, and also Roman-style baths. Perhaps these changes reflect the city's new name of Colonia Aurelia Augustana Antoniniana Felix Neapolis. Today, Latin has largely replaced Greek, and visitors will be hard pressed to find much Greek culture.

*Roman triremes can be seen in great numbers at Misenum, the headquarters of the Roman navy.*

## SURRENTUM

Surrentum overlooks its harbor on the southeastern shore of the Bay of Neapolis. Beneath the town lies a labyrinth of passages, stairs, and even roads accessing the villas built out from the cliffs and along the shore. The views from here across the bay to Neapolis, Puteoli, and Baiae are magnificent.

## THE ISLANDS

Procida (Pithecussae, in Greek) was the first place of Greek settlement—today it is a prison island. Meanwhile, Capreae (Capri) became the emperor's personal possession under Augustus, and it was to here that Tiberius retreated from Rome.

The cliff on the left-hand side of the island is reputed to have been the point from which astrologers were cast when they failed to predict their own deaths. The largest island is Aenaria (Ischia), which suffers from earthquakes, but boasts fine thermal baths.

## TRAVEL ON THE BAY OF NEAPOLIS

It is possible to take a boat to most destinations, but do not abandon your carriage until you have taken the road between Puteoli and Neapolis that runs through tunnels built by Cocceius.

# NORTHERN ITALY

THE JOURNEY FROM ROME TO MEDIOLANUM (MILAN) IS NOT A DIFFICULT ONE, BUT IT IS LONG AND CAN TAKE UP TO TWO WEEKS. THIS IS, HOWEVER, TIME WELL SPENT, AS IT WILL HELP YOU GAIN A FULL APPRECIATION OF THE VARIED LANDSCAPES OF ITALY, AND ALSO GIVE YOU THE CHANCE TO SEE SOME OF THE PLACES THAT WERE THE BASTIONS OF THE ROMAN EMPIRE DURING ITS TIME OF EXPANSION HALF A MILLENNIUM AGO.

### THE VIA FLAMINIA

The road that leaves Rome to the north across the Mulvian Bridge is over 500 years old, but is beautifully engineered and has been well maintained. You rise up onto the ridge of hills that run on the western side of the Tiber, much higher than the flood plain below, and where the road crosses valleys there are bridges and viaducts.

It is some 44 miles from here to Otricoli, where the road meets the Tiber. The city is a major river port with an amphitheater, theater, temples, and a fine set of modern baths. Rest here for the night, before leaving early to continue along the road to the bridge leading to Narnia; it was built by Augustus and is simply remarkable.

*The Mulvian Bridge dates back over five centuries,*
*providing an impressive example of Roman engineering.*

*The arch that marks the end of the Via Flaminia at Rimini.*

Take the right-hand fork and travel through Interamnia to Spalatum (Split), where it is worth resting prior to crossing the Apennines.

You need to leave early the next day to cover the 45 miles to Helvillum, where you can rest, overlooking the plain bounded by mountains, before setting out the following day to cross them.

The road from here is cut from the side of the hills and travels through several tunnels. Once you begin to descend you will be rewarded with views of the Adriatic Sea and the coastal plain.

The next day, set out across the plain for the colony at Pisaurum (Pisero), some 24 miles distant, with its remarkable walls established by Augustus. You may stop here or can head on for Ariminum (Rimini) where most travelers choose to break their journey. In any case there is much to see in Ariminum, a colony founded five and a half centuries ago close to the Rubicon. The river is famous for being crossed by caesar's legions some 350 years ago, and it was upon its north bank that he paused before stating "Alea iacta est" ("the die is cast") and signaling his men to advance toward civil war and the resulting downfall of the republic.

Recently much work has been done to rebuild the defenses of Ariminum. The port is remarkable, with canal and river connections through the marshes that form the estuary of the River Padus (Po). You might also visit the marshes, by boat or by road, within which lies the town of Ravenna.

## TO MEDIOLANUM

Leaving Ariminum via the bridge built by the emperor Tiberius, you follow the Via Aemilia. The road is dead straight. The Appenines rise on your left; on your right an unending vision of regular fields stretches across to the horizon. This is a totally Roman landscape: drained, surveyed, and divided, with towns established on a straight road 450 years ago.

Today the wealth lies here, in the north, and this has been the case for some 300 years. It is possible to reach Placentia (Piacenza) in four days, but visitors should visit some of the other cities on the road.

A day further on down the road is Faventia. Constructed on a grid, the city has grown due to the number of travelers on the road; while a further 34 miles on you will come to a similar settlement called Forum Cornelii, where the facilities are adequate for an overnight stay.

Bononia (Bologna) is your next port of call (25 miles further on),

*The baths of Hercules in Mediolanum house a colossal statue of the demi-god.*

a colony founded a little under 500 years ago on land taken from the Boii, but only really developed under Augustus. Little has been built recently, but the older sanctuary of Isis justifies a break in your journey.

Next is Parma, a colony settled six years after Bononia by 2,000 families. The city is famous for its manufacture of purple dye, but also offers good amenities including a theater and amphitheater.

A further 38 miles on is Placentia (Piacenza), a colony founded on the banks of the Padus (Po) at Rome's frontier with Gaul—although it soon needed to be refounded, as settlers had fled in the face of the enemy. The town was sacked and burnt to the ground in the civil wars following the suicide of Nero; however, it has since emerged as a major center of trade.

Just 44 miles north lies your destination: Mediolanum, the capital of the Roman West.

## THE NEW CAPITAL

Today, the center of power is here in Mediolanum (Milan). It is the new capital and will soon surpass even Rome in the number of magnificent sights that may be seen, while the city walls have recently been expanded and reinforced.

### RETURNING TO ROME

If your long journey to Mediolanum has tired you, then why not take a short cut on your return to Rome? It is possible to take a boat down the Padus and via the canals from Placentia to Rimini. The journey time depends greatly on the season and the flow of water in this mighty river.

Maximian is resident here and has built a splendid palace. The baths of Hercules are truly incredible, as is the hero's colossal statue housed inside.

Many have flocked to the city, including notables such as the leading Greek doctors, and the city has grown. Gladiatorial games are held in the amphitheater, plays put on in the theater, and chariot races take place in the circus. It is as though Rome has relocated to Mediolanum, and the offices of the governors of the provinces of Italy, Africa, and Illyricum are all located here. This is truly the capital of the Roman West, even if the senate still meets in Rome.

# SEA VOYAGES FROM ROME

FEW REALIZE QUITE HOW CLOSE ROME IS TO OTHER CITIES ON THE COAST OF THE MEDITERRANEAN. WITH THE RIGHT CURRENTS AND FAVORABLE WINDS, TRAVEL BY SEA CAN BE MUCH FASTER THAN BY ROAD. HOWEVER, THERE IS ALWAYS THE RISK OF BEING BLOWN OFF-COURSE AND WRECKED, SO THE LESS-ADVENTUROUS TRAVELER MAY PREFER TO TRAVEL BY LAND.

## CARTHAGE

Carthage, seven days' voyage away, was once Rome's great rival. Destroyed by the Romans, the city was refounded by Julius Caesar and has since emerged as the empire's second city. Colonia Iulia Concordia Karthago now boasts a splendid circus, harbor, baths, and two theaters. The most interesting site is the sanctuary of Tanit, as it was here that the Carthaginians sacrificed their own children. Worship of Juno Caelestis continues here today. Twice a year the cult statue is paraded and immersed in sea-water, both at the festival known as the Fercula and at the Procession of the Prostitutes.

## LEPTIS MAGNA

Leptis Magna, again a seven-day voyage from Rome, has long been a city of some importance; but, when Septimius Severus seized the throne just over a hundred years ago, it was embellished to resemble Rome itself.

The harbor is impressive, and from here visitors should take the colonnaded street—notice the 360 or so columns of marble—that leads to the new forum. The old forum is also worth a visit, as is the theater with its displays of sculpture. You will also find a circus and an amphitheater, all at the apogee of craftsmanship and architectural design.

*The arch of Septimius Severus in Leptis Magna.*

WHAT TO EXPECT

# LIFE ONBOARD

There is no such thing as a passenger vessel, but most trading vessels in Portus do take passengers. You will need to take your own food and servants, and be prepared to sleep in a tent on deck, while chairs are provided for the daytime. Be warned: storms are not infrequent, and can be terrifying even in the most seaworthy of vessels.

Some captains insist that passengers provide the funds for the customary sacrifice prior to departure, and also for that which is made onboard once the ship has arrived safely at its destination.

## ALEXANDRIA AND EGYPT

The voyage to Egypt is recommended to young men suffering from diseases and breathing difficulties.

Once in Alexandria, you will see a wondrous port with its lighthouse and the massive warehouses for storing grain prior to its transportation to Rome.

The population is split between Greeks and Jews, and the city is often rocked by sectarian violence. There is much to see here, the temple of Serapis being a major attraction, while the illuminated streets are another.

Many of the greatest minds in the world congregate here, as the libraries are exceptional, and you are sure to stumble across astronomers, astrologers, doctors, and mathematicians. Most visitors take this opportunity to travel up the Nile and see Egypt's former glories—but note that you need to apply to the governor for permission, and pay a fee.

## ATHENS AND GREECE

Greece has been off-limits until relatively recently, due to the Gothic invaders. However, it is once again possible to visit Athens and other famous cities.

The impact of Hadrian can be seen everywhere in Athens, as it was under his instructions that much of the city was redeveloped in an attempt to modernize it.

To reach Greece take the Via Appia to Brundisium (Brindisi) and make the short crossing to Dyrrachium.

**4**

# ENTERTAINMENT
# ON A BUDGET

*There is something for everyone in Rome. Whatever
time of year you visit, there will be festivals, plays,
gladiatorial combats, and chariot racing. You will
really feel alive in this city of so many festivals. In
theory these occasions honor the gods, but in fact they
are just as much occasions for feasting, spectacles, and
entertainment. Enjoy this city, it is like no other—
much pleasure awaits you in Rome.*

### VENARI LAVARI

### LUDERE RIDERE

### HOC EST VIVERE

*(Hunting, bathing, playing, laughing, that is living.)*

# FESTIVALS

 THERE ARE SO MANY FESTIVALS IN ROME THAT EVERY SO OFTEN A COMMISSION CONVENES TO ABOLISH SOME; MOST OF THEM WERE SET UP IN FLATTERY OF SOME PRETENDER TO THE THRONE OR OTHER. BECAUSE OF THIS PROLIFERATION ANY VISITOR TO ROME CAN BE SURE TO ENCOUNTER AT LEAST ONE FESTIVAL, AND PROBABLY MANY MORE.

**CALENDAR OF FESTIVALS**
Some traditional festivals date right back to the dawn of the republic, and even beyond to the time of Romulus. However, over the years many more have been added, and to avoid confusion it is advisable to refer to a calendar of their exact dates—you can find an inscribed copy at the local *compitum* (crossroads) held by the *vici magistri* (magistrates of the neighborhood). Some of the more notable festivals are listed here:

---

**JANUARY**

| | |
|---|---|
| New Year's Day | Consuls process to the Capitol |
| Ludi Compitales | Boxing and games in the neighborhoods |

**FEBRUARY**

| | |
|---|---|
| Fornacalia | Feast of ovens held across the city |
| Parentalia | Festival of the dead at family tombs |
| Lupercalia | Fertility festival |
| Equirria | Festival of horse racing |

**MARCH**

| | |
|---|---|
| Argei | Procession of the puppets (*Argei*) |
| Liberalia | Coming-of-age festival for boys |

**APRIL**

| | |
|---|---|
| Ludi Megalenses | Games of Magna Mater or Cybele |
| Ludi Cereri | Games of Ceres |
| Fordicidia | Pregnant cows sacrificed |

---

Parilia — Celebrates the birth of Rome
Vinalia — Festival of the vintage
Ludi Florae — Games with performances by prostitutes
Feriae Conceptivae — The Latin festival

## MAY
Bona Dea — Fertility festival, for women only
Laribus — Festival of the Lares (guardian spirits)
Lemuria — Appeasing of the *lemures* (ghosts)
Mars Invictus — Festival of the Invincible War God
Argei — Puppets cast into the Tiber
Mercury and Maia — Festival in Circus Maximus

## JUNE
Ludi Piscatorii — Fishermen's games on the Tiber
Matralia — Festival of Mothers
Quinquatrus — Festival of Flute Players

## JULY
Ludi Apollinares — Games of Apollo
Ancillarum feriae — Feast of slave girls
Equitum Romanorum — Procession of the Equites (Knights)

## AUGUST
Vinalia — Wine festival
Consualia — Harvest Festival

## SEPTEMBER
Ludi Romani — The Roman Games—oldest of the games

## OCTOBER
Ludi Capitolini — Games of Jupiter

## NOVEMBER
Ludi Plebeii — Games of the Plebs

## DECEMBER
Bona Dea — Women's festival
Saturnalia — Winter Festival—gambling and feasting

# A DAY AT THE RACES

ONE OF THE MOST THRILLING EXPERIENCES TO BE HAD
IN ROME IS JOINING THE 250,000 SPECTATORS IN THE
CIRCUS MAXIMUS TO WATCH THE CHARIOTS CAREEN AROUND
THE TRACK. HERE YOU MAY BET ON THE DRIVER OR COLOR
OF YOUR CHOICE, MINGLE WITH THE LOCALS, AND EVEN FLIRT
WITH OTHER SPECTATORS. YOU WILL SEE SKILLED DRIVING,
HORSES OF EXCEPTIONAL SPEED, AND THE LARGEST CROWD
ON EARTH. A MEMORABLE EXPERIENCE INDEED!

In the Circus Maximus seating is less controlled than in the theaters or amphitheaters; men and women can sit together, and people of differing status mingle freely. All are consumed by the passion of the occasion.

There are four teams, identified by color: the Blues, Greens, Reds, and Whites. The events commence in the morning with a religious procession of images of the gods, followed by the charioteers. The first race is often the most exciting, as only experienced drivers compete, but throughout the day you will see chariots drawn by two horses (driven by novices), three horses, four horses (the most common), and even six horses.

Competitors line up in 12 starting gates, and each of the four teams may present three chariots and their drivers for a race. Races take place over seven laps, covering about five Roman miles in total, and the action is fast and furious with as many as three races held an hour, and 24 in a day.

The charioteer stands erect in his colored tunic with whip in hand; he also has a knife to cut himself free, should there be a crash. You may also see riders perform tricks on horses, and perhaps some foot races as well, but these are simply sideshows to the main event.

*A chariot crash at
the Circus Maximus.*

---

## LIVING FAST

One of the most successful charioteers, P. Aelius Gutta Calpurnianus, favored African horses. And having won a total of 1,127 races—78 for the reds, 102 for the whites, 364 for the greens, and 583 for the blues—he even managed to survive into retirement.

Crescens was another successful charioteer. He hailed from Mauritania and began racing when he was thirteen, going on to win an impressive 1,558,346 sesterces in prize money. However, his death in a chariot crash at the age of 22 stands as a monument to the fate that awaits many of the young men who pursue wealth and glory in this way.

---

### RACING KNOWLEDGE

The bars of Rome house fierce debates about the merits of each team, the pedigree of individual horses, and the skill of drivers. In short, Romans are obsessed with chariot racing. Successful drivers become celebrities, made rich through their winnings—as each race is sponsored—and can earn a hundred times what an accomplished lawyer might. Prizes as high as 50,000 sesterces for one race are not unknown.

---

WHAT TO EXPECT

## GAMBLING AT THE RACES

The atmosphere of excitement in the circus is multiplied by the fact that many of the 250,000 spectators have money riding on the outcome of the races. This is big business, but betting remains informal, with no bookmakers as such. Punters bet on a color rather than an individual chariot or driver, and with the Blues and Greens pre-eminent even odds can be obtained on their relative performances, as well as those of the Whites and Reds paired to one or other of the more successful teams. If you bet sensibly the odds are that you will break even over the course of 24 races.

# GLADIATORIAL COMBATS AND BEAST HUNTS

EVERYWHERE YOU GO IN THE ROMAN WORLD, YOU WILL FIND GLADIATORS. EVEN IN SMALL TOWNS SUCH AS CARMARTHEN, AT THE OUTERMOST EDGES OF THE EMPIRE, YOU WILL FIND AN AMPHITHEATER TO PLAY HOST TO THEIR BATTLES—ALTHOUGH MANY ARE NOW DERELICT. IN ROME, HOWEVER, YOU WILL STILL FIND THE LARGEST AMPHITHEATER OF ALL, THE COLOSSEUM.

Shows have been put on in Rome for more than 500 years and the enthusiasm of the Romans for them is as strong as ever. In spite of the political and military instability of the last century, the import of wild beasts and their slaughter has continued unabated. The senators pay for them, and call in favors from contacts in the provinces to deliver such exotic creatures as antelopes, bears and cubs, crocodiles, hippos, as well as lions and other felines.

When the Colosseum was opened under the emperor Titus, over 200 years ago, some 5,000 animals were slaughtered, setting the benchmark for the spectacles that followed. The emperor Trajan gave such lavish games, with 11,000 wild animals and 10,000 gladiators, that they lasted 123 days.

### GLADIATORS

Gladiators are equipped with a wide variety of arms and armor. Most wear helmets, apart from the *retiarius* (netman), but these serve not so much for defense as to hinder the sphere of vision.

---

WHAT TO EXPECT

## SOUVENIRS

There are numerous gladiator trinkets to be brought in Rome: lamps with gladiators on them; figurines; and most strangely, wind-chimes featuring a gladiator slashing with his *gladius* at his penis as it metamorphoses into a lion—a unique souvenir that is explained by the fact that the word *gladius* refers both to a sword and the penis.

*The lives of gladiators are short and bloody, but they are vaunted as heroes while they live and fight.*

A common pairing is the *secutor*—protected and hindered by a large shield, a single metal greave, and a helmet with tiny eye-holes—and the lightly armed but more mobile retiarius, who fights with a trident and a net. The variety of weaponry makes this game of death far more interesting to the Romans than other blood sports such as boxing.

---

WHAT TO EXPECT

## SEATING IN THE COLOSSEUM

When you have found your seat, you will gaze over the 50,000 spectators awaiting the start; those in front of you are your betters, those behind your inferiors. You will witness a beast show in the morning, and the gladiatorial contests in the afternoon, while the lunch break features the execution of condemned criminals. The skill on show is what attracts many visitors to the games, but the frenzy of death that unfolds below you makes it hard not to become caught up in the bloodlust of the crowd and join in with the inevitable cries of "Kill him!"

# AQUATIC ENTERTAINMENT

MANY VISITORS ARRIVE IN ROME EXPECTING TO SEE AQUATIC DISPLAYS BEING HELD IN THE COLOSSEUM. THIS IS FRANKLY NONSENSE, BUT PERSISTENT RUMORS CONTINUE TO HAVE CREDENCE AMONG THOSE WHO HAVE NOT VISITED ROME FOR THEMSELVES. AT THE MOMENT, RE-ENACTMENTS OF SEA BATTLES SEEM TO HAVE BECOME A THING OF THE PAST, BUT THERE ARE RUMORS THAT THEY MIGHT REAPPEAR UNDER DIOCLETIAN AND MAXIMIAN, WHO ARE AFTER ALL THE RESTORERS OF MANY TRADITIONS.

## THE NAUMACHIAE

There are two venues on which sea fights and aquatic displays have been held in the past. The most famous is the one built by Augustus in Transtiberim and supplied with water from the Aqua Alsietina. The basin measures 1,800 by 1,200 Roman feet and it is possible for it to host a re-enactment featuring up to 30 ships—a water-filled arena almost as large as the Circus Maximus, on which has been staged a re-enactment of the Battle of Salamis. Today, it is possible to make out the remains of this once splendid structure that is now bisected by the city wall. It was last used to celebrate the millennium of the city under the emperor Philip.

Events have also been held on the stagnum (lake) of Agrippa on the Campus Martius. This was the location of the famous party of Nero, organized by the praetorian prefect Tigellinus—a banquet for all the people of Rome with rafts and boats, every marine creature, and brothels along the shoreline in which the wives of the prominent acted as prostitutes, while the beach was filled with naked prostitutes.

## PERFORMANCES

There is a range of spectacles on offer. In the pantomime of Nereids swimming in sync, these beautiful creatures appear like the sea nymphs of myth—but in fact they are prostitutes recruited from the brothels.

You can also see the myth of Leander re-enacted. As the criminal playing Leander makes his way to see his lover, the waves are made to crash and his prayer, "Spare me while I'm hurrying to her, drown me on the way back," is made true for many criminals.

Beast hunts are also held in the waters, and as many as 5,000

animals have been slaughtered in the course of a single day's entertainment.

## VENUES OUTSIDE ROME

For the visitor who ventures beyond Rome, the Bay of Neapolis (see pp.88–9) is the natural arena for sea fights and the staging of aquatic displays. It was here that Caligula built his bridge of boats and drove across the sea in a chariot. Lakes and rivers have been used for the re-enactment of naval battles and the staging of banquets on rafts, both in Italy and much more recently in the provinces. The provincials in Gaul can imagine themselves in the landscape of the Bay of Neapolis, with the god Bacchus overseeing the drama acted out in front of an imaginary Mount Vesuvius.

The sea fights in these locations are much more similar to real contests, and the outcome is accordingly less certain. History can often be reversed—nothing is staged and the fighting is real. The Athenians may be overcome by the Persians in one night's Battle of Salamis, only to be defeated in the next showing of the same contest.

*Scantily clad nereids perform synchronized routines in the waters of the Naumachiae.*

# BATHS AND SPAS

BATHING IS THE SINGLE MOST IMPORTANT ROMAN INSTITUTION. IN A CRISIS ROMANS COULD FORSAKE THE AMPHITHEATER, THE CIRCUS, OR THE THEATER, BUT BATHING IS ESSENTIAL AND YOU CAN FIND BATHS IN EVEN THE MOST REMOTE FORTS AT THE VERY FRONTIERS OF CIVILIZATION. THE ROMANS HAVE INTRODUCED BATHING TO THE NORTHERN AND WESTERN PROVINCES, BUT OF COURSE IT IS IN ROME THAT YOU WILL FIND THE LARGEST, MOST SOPHISTICATED, AND MOST BEAUTIFUL BATHS IN THE WORLD.

There there is simply no excuse for the visitor to Rome to let his or her standards of personal hygiene slip. Not only are there many opportunities to bathe, but the use of perfume came to Rome from the Persians, and masses of flowers are grown in order to squeeze out drops of fragrant oil. These scents are used by both men and women, and small glass bottles of such fragrances can be purchased.

## BATHING

Bathing has featured in Roman life for at least 500 years. The first baths were small and dark, but with the development of window glass, double-glazed in some cases, the baths became lighter and more magnificent. The addition of glass mosaics, marble, statuary, and multiple pools has transformed the experience. As a result, bath buildings have become much more than just places to wash: there are libraries, gardens, running tracks, and you might even stumble across the odd philosopher.

Unsurprisingly, the new baths of Diocletian are set to be the largest yet when they are completed, but for the moment the earlier baths of Caracalla retain that distinction. You will find baths in every city and even in most villages in Italy.

It is not just a matter of cleanliness—the Romans believe that bathing is part of a regimen designed to maintain their good health. As such, the heating and cooling of the body is not just a pleasure, but a necessity.

*A small collection of perfume bottles.*

*When finally complete, the new baths of Diocletian
are expected to eclipse all others in scale and grandeur.*

## WHAT TO EXPECT

# GOING TO THE BATHS

When visiting the baths, first go to the changing room, undress, and pay the attendant to put oil on you. Now you need to exercise—ball games are perhaps the easiest to join in for first-timers. Then you should visit the warm room, bracing yourself for the full heat of the *caldarium* (hot room). It is a matter of choice at what point you have the dirt scraped off with a strigil, and there are options on the way for a cold plunge or a dip in the *piscina* (plunge pool). At the end of the process comes massage, optional depilation, and oiling of the body. The result is a clean and invigorated body.

The best time to go is in the eighth hour, when the baths are at a perfect temperature: neither ferociously hot, as they tend to be in the sixth hour, nor too cool, as in the tenth hour.

The Romans are not shy, and make no attempt to hide their nakedness. In fact, some baths offer mixed bathing, so the best advice is to shrug off your inhibitions and enjoy the experience.

# THEATERS

THE THEATER IS FOR THE ROMANS THE POOR RELATION OF THE
AMPHITHEATER AND THE CIRCUS, WITH SMALLER AUDIENCES
THAN EITHER. HOWEVER, IT STILL HAS ITS PLACE AND MANY
ACTORS HAVE ACHIEVED POPULARITY OR NOTORIETY, WHILE
THE LUDI (GAMES) INCLUDE EVENTS IN THE THEATER AS
WELL AS IN THE CIRCUS.

Plays are staged as part of the games, and traditionally they explain or develop the mythical story associated with the festival being celebrated—such as the Ludi *scaenici* (plays) that are held in honor of Apollo, Flora, Cybele, and Jupiter Optimus Maximus. An interesting feature of a theater's role in these celebrations is the *lectisternium,* a spectacle in which images of the gods are brought from the temples to be present at the plays.

## WHAT TO SEE

The thespian tradition has developed a whole set of plays in Italy, known as Fabulae Atellanae. These use masks and stock characters with which the Greek comic traditions have been interwoven. These plays were brought to Rome and have largely supplanted the city's traditions of dance, which can sometimes still be seen when the *salii* (priests) dance through the streets, and in the use of masks in Roman funerals.

*A Roman play in full swing.*

## A Play to End all Plays

When Pompey dedicated his theater, he had a performance of *Clytemnestra* by the playwright Accius put on. In order to do justice to its grand surroundings, so great was the production that 600 mules were employed to carry the booty brought back from Troy by Agamemnon.

Many plays pander to the base demands of the crowds; and those that form part of the games sacred to Florus, the Floralia, feature full nudity, in which the performers are prostitutes rather than actors.

Pantomime has also been popular for some time, and features the usual pratfalls and clowning around, often in the guise of mythical characters; for example, an actor portraying Hercules as a drunk will caper about in the most comic way. A Latin genre of farces also developed under the emperor Domitian, of which the play *Hercules the Debt Collector* is perhaps the most famous.

Visitors would be unlucky not to see a theatrical performance— there are as many as 40 days of Ludi Scaenici throughout the Roman year. However, they are not to everyone's tastes— Christian writers have denounced the shows, along with those in the amphitheaters and circuses. Perhaps the shows' pagan roots are not to their tastes, but their complaints do little more than secure their own unpopularity.

### NOTABLE THEATERS

The theater of Pompey is the largest stone theater in the empire, and was the first to be built in Rome. It is also the most beautiful. You can also catch performances at the theater of Marcellus, the theater of Balbus, and in the Odeon built by Domitian. All of these are located conveniently close to one another in the Campus Martius.

The century following the reign of Augustus saw theaters built in many cities in Italy and the West. There are also numerous theaters in the Gallic provinces, mostly not in the cities themselves but at their sanctuaries. Many are little more than a space for the performance to take place, with seating arranged in the fashion of that found in Rome, and they are often in need of repair and restoration. Neapolis (see pp.90–1), where Nero himself performed, still commands the greatest audiences and plays host to competitions in music, song, and dance.

# EATING AND DRINKING

VISITORS WILL FIND THAT ROMANS TEND TO EAT DINNER
AT THE NINTH HOUR OF THE DAY, AND SIMPLY SNACK AT
NOON. THE POPINAE (BARS) OF THE CITY CATER FOR THESE
DEMANDS, OFFERING A RANGE OF COLD SNACKS AND THE
OCCASIONAL PASTRY. THE SALE OF COOKED MEAT FROM
THESE ESTABLISHMENTS IS TECHNICALLY PROHIBITED, BUT IN
PRACTICE THIS IS NOT ENFORCED.

*Nine diners recline in
an intimate dining room.*

Although reclining for dinner was originally a Greek custom, it has been present in Italy for hundreds of years. However, much has changed, and today you can expect to find a *stibadium* (a semi-circular dining couch) rather than the traditional arrangement of three couches for nine diners.

The stibadium will be sited in an apse, and in front of this "high table" other diners will be seated in the hall—these are persons of lower status: clients, freedmen, and even important slaves of the owner. The stibadium will be well lit by lamps, whereas the rest of the hall will be gloomy. The right-hand end is the seat of honor, while the diner at the left-hand end is there for entertainment—expect them to recite their own poems or even provide a panegyric speech that praises the host while apologizing for an earlier slight or misdemeanor.

# A TRADITIONAL DINNER

If you receive a dinner invitation, you should arrive prior to the ninth hour. You will be admitted to the atrium and have the chance, with the other guests, to admire the decoration. You can expect a pre-dinner reception in the library, before entering the dining room.

There will probably be a total of nine diners spread over three couches or across a stibadium. You should recline and wait to be served by your host's slaves. There may be some form of entertainment, and there will certainly be intellectual conversation.

As a visitor to Rome your host is sure to quiz you about your travels, but don't be too offended should he ask questions that seem designed to make you appear foolish. Such questioning is intended to enhance the status of your host, albeit at your expense, and even the emperor Tiberius loved to ask such teasingly impossible questions as: "What was Achilles called when he dressed as a woman?"

---

Should you feel sick during the course of a dinner—perhaps as a result of eating or drinking too much—you should not worry unduly. It is not uncommon, and being sick is actually regarded as an aid to good health; however, it is polite to ask a slave to aid you.

After dinner, Romans will pull out their *dentiscalpium* (toothpick) or *auriscalpium* (earpick) and set to work.

## DRINKING

Drinking alcohol is considered essential at dinner. In fact, the Romans also introduced drinking on an empty stomach 300 years ago, and the practice persists. Should you be invited to such a party, you should be aware that vomiting is not uncommon. There is no discreet place to do this, but it is nevertheless best to call a slave to help you to an appropriate distance from your host.

Away from such unruly surroundings, Romans mix their wine with hot or cold water. It can also be sweetened, with honey by the rich or with lead sulfide by the poor. A vast array of wines is available from throughout Italy and all over the Mediterranean.

# SEX AND THE BROTHELS OF ROME

VISITORS NEED TO BE AWARE THAT ROMAN LAW IS QUITE PRESCRIPTIVE WHEN IT COMES TO THE QUESTION OF WITH WHOM A MAN OR WOMAN MAY HAVE SEX. IF YOU ARE MALE, ANY FEMALE PARTNER SHOULD NOT BE MARRIED, NOR BE AN UNMARRIED VIRGIN, WHILE MALE PARTNERS NEED TO CONSENT. IF YOU ARE FEMALE, YOU SHOULD IDEALLY BE MARRIED TO YOUR MALE PARTNER, AND THE LAW DOES NOT RECOGNIZE THE POSSIBILITY OF FEMALE PARTNERS. HOWEVER, AS IN OTHER SOCIETIES, THE LAW DOES NOT REFLECT ALL OF THE PRACTICES OF THE PEOPLE, ALTHOUGH WHATEVER YOUR INCLINATIONS IT PAYS TO BE CAUTIOUS.

Many Roman men, including emperor Maximian, find both teenage boys as well as girls sexually attractive; however, the idea of sex with an older man or a man of similar age is considered abhorrent by most Romans. Such men are referred to as *cinaedi*— sexually passive males, who seek to give other men pleasure, rather than seeking their own.

Roman women are thought of, by men at least, as being sexually passive, particularly in marriage.

---

WHAT TO EXPECT

## A ROMAN BROTHEL

Should you choose to visit a Roman brothel, you should not expect any great comfort. The entrance hall will be lit, and from it you will see a series of rooms each shielded by a curtain. The picture over the entrance to each room gives a rough idea of what takes place within. You may well have to wait your turn. While waiting, you may discuss your desires with the pimp, who may be male or female, or even pass the time reading the graffiti for recommendations or criticism.

*Brothels are far from luxurious,
indeed they are often decidedly cramped.*

However, it should be pointed out that Roman history is littered with sexually active women—particularly those in their thirties who had given birth to children—the emperor Augustus' daughter, Julia, being the most famous.

## PROSTITUTION

Male and female prostitutes throughout the empire, as well as their pimps, are regulated and required to pay a tax—a levy introduced by the emperor Caligula. The sum raised is quite considerable and is said to have funded Alexander Severus' restoration of the circus, amphitheater, and theaters. Freeborn Romans are not permitted to marry prostitutes, although it is worth noting that the law does not consider a married man having sex with a prostitute to be an act of adultery; however, should his wife indulge in the same exploits it would be considered a most scandalous act, and one that is quite against the law.

The number of prostitutes is reflected in the importance of the tax to the treasury, and it is a business that has continued to flourish. The cost of a prostitute varies greatly, but the majority are relatively cheap—about the price of a few cups of wine. Alexander Severus considered making male prostitution illegal, but rejected the idea on the grounds that this would just be counterproductive—simply pushing the trade out of sight of the city's authorities.

# PRACTICAL
# CONSIDERATIONS

*Although visitors to Rome should find much useful
information in the following pages, it should be noted
that circumstances are liable to change at short notice.
This is particularly the case at the current time: this
material was updated in the sixteenth year of
Diocletian's reign, when potential changes to the
pricing of goods and a revaluation or reform of the
coinage were under consideration.*

# How to Get There

WHETHER TRAVELING BY SEA OR OVERLAND, YOUR PROGRESS IS BOUND TO BE RATHER UNPREDICTABLE, AND YOU CAN NEVER BE QUITE SURE WHEN YOU MIGHT ARRIVE AT YOUR DESTINATION. HOWEVER, TO TRAVEL BY LAND IS GENERALLY CONSIDERED THE SAFER OPTION OF THE TWO.

### THE PORTS OF ITALY

There is a number of landing points in Italy, convenient for visitors from many different nations. Once landfall is made, travelers can use the famous roads that lead across Italy to Rome. The following list of ports is provided for travel information:

**Ancona**—convenient for travelers from the Balkans.

**Brundisium (Brindisi)**—the closest port to Greece on the Via Appia.

**Genoa**—convenient for travelers from Gaul.

**Portus**—the closest port to Rome; take Via Portuensis to enter the city.

**Puteoli**—on the Bay of Neapolis.

**Rhegium**—the closest port to Sicily.

**Ariminum**—on the Adriatic coast, convenient for travel down the River Padus or on the Via Flaminia.

### APPROACHING OVERLAND

Because Rome is spread over seven hills, you will be able to see the city from a considerable distance.

Those coming from the south will climb the Alban Hills and see the city laid out before them on the plain, with roads and aqueducts crossing the countryside to converge on the city.

Those coming from the north will gradually make the descent from the rolling hills of Etruria before crossing the Mulvian Bridge over the Tiber to enter the city.

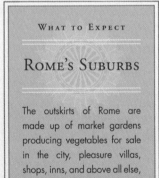

WHAT TO EXPECT

## ROME'S SUBURBS

The outskirts of Rome are made up of market gardens producing vegetables for sale in the city, pleasure villas, shops, inns, and above all else, cemeteries. The Romans are not allowed to bury their dead in the city, and outside every city along the roads you will find tombs in various shapes and sizes, from simple *stelae* to pyramids.

*The Via Appia passes endless rows of tombs as you descend towards Rome.*

## ROADS LEADING TO ROME

**Via Appia  Via Amerina** from Amelia

**Via Aurelia** from Genoa

**Via Cassia** from Etruria

**Via Clodia** from Etruria

**Via Flaminia** from Ariminum

**Via Latina** from Capua

**Via Ostiensis** from Ostia

**Via Portuensis** from Portus

**Via Salaria** from Reate

Those traveling from Portus or along the coast road (the Via Aurelia) will enter the city via Transtiberim.

Whichever way you come, you will know when you are nearing the city by your view of the skyline of temples and the increasing number of cemeteries that you see as you approach the city.

# GETTING AROUND

ONCE YOU'VE MADE YOUR WAY TO ROME YOU WILL NEED TO
NEGOTIATE ITS MANY STREETS; HOWEVER, IN SPITE OF THE
MAGNIFICENT NETWORK OF ROADS THAT SPANS THE COUNTRY,
THE CITY ITSELF IS NOT THE EASIEST TO TRAVEL THROUGH.

### IN ROME

Wheeled vehicles are banned from the city from dawn until the ninth hour of the day, with the important exception of vehicles used in religious processions and the innumerable number of wagons that supply the building sites of the emperors' new works and restoration projects.

As a result, you will need to travel on foot or be carried in a litter. It is suggested that visitors hire a litter and litter bearers for the duration of their stay in Rome, and use this facility to transport them to and from where they wish to visit. If you travel early, before the second hour, the streets are less busy than later in the day. After the ninth hour, Rome is full of vehicles bringing in bulkier supplies and congestion is a frequent problem. Goods are also delivered to shops

WHAT TO EXPECT

## A ROMAN LITTER

A litter is a relatively large and comfortable means of travel, if a rather slow one—in crowded streets, litter bearers can often simply find no way through, and if numerous litters are using the street then congestion is likely. A litter has enough space for two adults to travel with ease, and its motion is even said to abate some health problems (just as the shaking from rides in chariots or the motion of a sea voyage is thought to be beneficial). The curtains of the litter can be kept open so that you can see the streets of Rome from above the crowds, or be closed for your privacy.

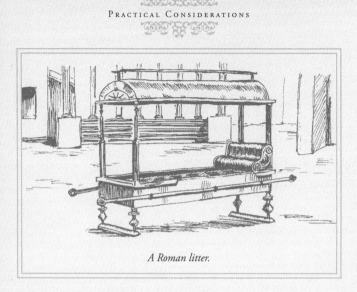

*A Roman litter.*

on pack animals: donkeys and mules. If you are planning any major purchases, you may wish to hire a donkey for the day, with its attendant; but most traders in Rome can arrange for your goods to be delivered (charges are made: a donkey load will cost 4 denarii per mile).

## ON THE OPEN ROAD

You can get a ride on a cart at less than 2 denarii per mile. There are several things to do to pass the time: you might employ a slave to read extracts from the historians—Livy on the republic or Tacitus on the early empire, or a writer on more recent times; or you can use this time to compose letters, or poems, or jot down your memories of the sites of Rome.

The speed of travel should be estimated at between 20 and 35 miles per day for leisurely journeys, but you can increase this to 45 or 50 miles a day if the roads are clear and you hurry.

You will inevitably arrive at your destination weary, however, because although the Romans make use of much wonderful technology, they do not use springs to cushion the jolting of your carriage's wheels.

Once you have found your accommodation, head for the baths—you will get clean and your body will begin to recover from the rigors of your day's travel. The baths are also marvelous places to watch the local inhabitants, as they go about their ablutions, and get a real feel for the place you are staying in even if only overnight.

# ACCOMMODATION

VISITORS TO ROME ARE FACED WITH A MASSIVE CHOICE OF
ACCOMMODATION, FROM RENTED ROOMS TO RENTED VILLAS
IN THE SUBURBS. MUCH DEPENDS ON YOUR BUDGET, BUT
EXPECT ALL ACCOMMODATION IN ROME TO BE SOME FOUR
TIMES MORE EXPENSIVE THAN IN THE PROVINCES. MOST
ROMANS RENT PROPERTY RATHER THAN OWN IT, AND
ONE MEANS OF SUPPLEMENTING THEIR INCOME IS BY SUB-
LETTING ROOMS TO OTHERS. IT IS WORTH NOTING THAT ALL
ACCOMMODATION WILL BE SCARCE AND EXPENSIVE WHEN
DIOCLETIAN OR MAXIMIAN VISITS THE CITY.

## CAUPONAE

*Cauponae* (inns) vary from basic bars with a few rooms, to fancy dining rooms arranged around a garden with rooms for hire in the upper stories. You can find cauponae in Rome, on the roads, and in other cities. There are numerous stories told of innkeepers murdering their guests, but these are exaggerated.

Many cauponae are not purpose-built and are the result of the subdivision of property. Many are owned by widows and provide a means for their support. You may have to provide your own food in some establishments. Some establishments provide prostitutes, in others the slaves run a minor sex industry on the

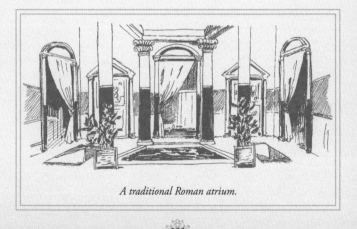

*A traditional Roman atrium.*

# LEGAL RESPONSIBILITIES OF TENANTS

Nothing must be made worse by your occupation of rented premises beyond reasonable wear and tear. Otherwise, the landlord is permitted to seize your goods as payment for repairs. You are also responsible for damages caused by your slaves and family, as well as the slaves and family of any guests you admit to the property. You need to check the contract as to whether you are permitted to have a fire or cook on the premises. Note that if you are unable to use all of the property as intended, it is possible to deduct monies from the rent. Finally, beware of landlords who narrow the entranceway, so that you are unable to remove your strongbox or newly purchased furniture when you leave.

side. Many inns have stabling and might provide fodder for draught animals at a price. Roman inns vary considerably; check for a good water supply, good locks, and a positive impression of both the proprietor and the other residents.

### RENTED APARTMENTS

A *cenaculum* or rented second-floor apartment comes with several rooms and suitable space for entertaining. How much you pay depends on the location of the apartment in the city. Closer to the forum is more expensive, as are apartments on the hills of Rome, especially the Aventine. Apartments on the upper floors of *insulae* (apartment blocks) tend to

be much cheaper to rent, but you will need to be good at climbing and jumping in the not entirely unimaginable event of a fire.

### RENTED HOUSES

If you have the money and wish to make an impact on polite society, you need to rent a *domus* (house). The classic atrium with peristyle does still exist in Rome, but you might wish to have more modern facilities such as a dining room with an apse and a curved dining couch.

Alternatively, you might wish to rent a villa on the coast south of Ostia or in the hills around Rome, for example at Tibur (Tivoli).

# CUSTOMS AND MANNERS

THE ROMANS MAINTAIN THAT MANY OF THEIR CUSTOMS
AND MANNERS DATE BACK TO THEIR FIRST KING, ROMULUS.
THERE IS ALSO A LONG TRADITION OF THE EMPERORS, FROM
AUGUSTUS ONWARD, RESTORING THE ANCIENT CUSTOMS OF
THE ROMANS.

### SLAVERY

Rome, outside the military establishment, is run by the power and intellect of its slaves. They are everywhere serving the interests of their owners, and many are freed as a reward for good service.

Most Romans who trace their ancestry honestly will find slavery in their bloodline. Slaves when freed become citizens, but they may continue to work for their former master, and they will almost certainly owe their former master certain duties. For an idea of the numbers of freed slaves, visit a cemetery—many of the largest tombs have been built by this group of new Romans.

### MARRIAGE

Men get married in their mid-to-late twenties, whereas girls are married off in their teens. Prior to marriage there is a period of betrothal, marked by gifts from the groom to his future wife; these used

*Slaves are sold at auction to the highest bidder.*

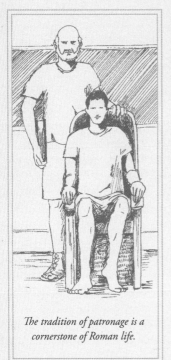

*The tradition of patronage is a cornerstone of Roman life.*

age are expected, under the laws of Augustus, to be married. There is an ideal of marriage for life, but in practice several marriage partners seems to be the modern norm.

## PATRONAGE

From the time of Romulus, the rich became patrons of the poor, their clients. You will see clients arriving at their patron's door from dawn for the *salutatio* or "getting up." They congregate in the hope of getting a gift, a recommendation, advice on the law or on any other matter. They troop behind their patron as he goes to the forum or the baths, and he is only released from this duty at the end of the day.

## WOMEN AND CHILDREN

Women do not have the same rights as men. Throughout their lives they have a male *tutor* (guardian), who grants them permission for their public actions. The reason women are thought to need such a tutor is that they may own much property, but are not thought to have the necessary expertise to make any decisions regarding its use.

to be just a ring, but have grown in number to numerous gold rings and other jewelry. It is easy to spot the betrothed girl wearing her gifts or insignia of betrothal.

Marriage involves a procession to the new house, with obscene songs and shouts. Marriages can be ended with divorce, which is often due to infertility. All men between the ages of 25 and 60 and all women 20 to 50 years of

Similarly, males under the age of 25 are not thought to have the maturity to deal with their own financial and legal affairs. For this reason all are subject to guardianship, if their father is no longer alive.

# CLOTHING AND DRESS

THERE IS A FAMOUS LINE: "BEHOLD THE TOGA-CLAD ROMANS, RULERS OF THE WORLD." CONTRARY TO POPULAR BELIEF, THE ROMANS DO NOT WEAR THE TOGA ALL THE TIME. PUBLIC MEETINGS AND OTHER OFFICIAL OCCASIONS— SACRIFICES, COMING-OF-AGE CEREMONIES, BETROTHALS, MARRIAGE CEREMONIES, FUNERALS, AND OTHER SUCH EVENTS—ARE TIMES TO WEAR THIS GARMENT.

## THE HISTORY OF THE TOGA

The toga has changed in its design over the years from its adoption as the dress of the kings of Rome. It originates from Etruria.

Under the republic it became a badge of citizenship to be worn on official occasions. You can see its shape in Augustus' time on the Ara Pacis (altar of Augustan Peace):

*A Roman in his toga.*

a flowing garment that was draped over the man's tunic down to his ankles. It is said that the orator Cicero began the fashion for long togas, due to a need to cover his prominent varicose veins.

Orators need well-tailored togas that highlight their physique; it is said that a famous orator, Hortensius, sued a man who bumped into him and caused his toga to become disarranged. The emperor Augustus insisted that all citizens wore the garment at official meetings and sacrifices; dark clothes are considered unlucky on these occasions, hence the whiteness of the toga.

Today the toga is shorter in length and stops just below the knee. Men tend to wear a loincloth beneath their tunic.

## FEMALE DRESS

If the toga is a man's official dress, the *stola* is a Roman woman's. It identifies her as a respectable citizen who, unlike slave women

*A Roman woman's stola.*

women might wear a breastband and briefs whilst exercising. Women also wear leggings.

### JEWELRY

Roman history is filled with women bedecked in jewels. Lollia Paulina, Caligula's wife, went about in public always covered in emeralds, pearls, and every manner of jewel on her head, in her hair, on her neck, on her ears, and on her fingers.

### THE EMPEROR'S NEW CLOTHES

Many emperors past have insisted on wearing the clothes of a citizen—Septimius Severus was praised for his simple dress and lack of purple, while Alexander Severus wore plain clothes and little gold. However, Gallienus began a new trend for jewels, gold, and purple cloaks. Perhaps this is a more honest reflection of the emperor's elevated status, and indeed when Diocletian visits Rome his dress will always set him apart and reflect his position.

and prostitutes, is immune from sexual harassment. Today, women wear short-sleeved tunics under the stola, but there is also a long-sleeved version. Over the tunic a *palla* or mantle is draped. The effect of draped clothing is to distinguish men from women.

Beneath a woman's tunic lies her breastband—a strip of cloth to augment the shape of the breasts. At the baths, you will find that

## SHOULD YOU WEAR A TOGA?

Only Roman citizens may wear the toga, so if you are not a citizen do not wear a toga in public. Women should not wear a toga under any circumstances, as this is the garb of a female prostitute.

# FOOD AND DRINK

THERE IS SO MUCH FOOD TO TRY AND SO MANY DIFFERENT WINES; ALL THE PRODUCE OF THE MEDITERRANEAN CONVERGES ON ROME. THERE IS AN IMMENSE VARIETY OF FOODS BOTH FAMILIAR AND UNFAMILIAR.

Food in Rome is not all stuffed dormice—in fact it offers interesting blends of flavors in most dishes.

Apicius' cookbook provides a good guide to the variations to be found. A chicken salad will include bread, pine kernels, cheese, sweetbreads, a whole range of spices, and have snow scattered over the top. Honeyed mushrooms, you may be surprised to find, contain garum (fish sauce). There is a range of soups—suitable for the visitor on a budget—that are based around vegetables, barley, and lentils. Note that the Romans adore lentils and consider them to promote an even temper.

Moving on from this simple fare are casseroles. Every type of bird available, including ostrich, is served with a range of sauces; just as every quadruped seems to be roasted, boiled, or marinated in sea water and served with a variety of spicy or sweet sauces.

When near the coast, eat fresh seafood or farmed oysters—Rome tends to have some pretty dubious fish on sale. There are good farmed lampreys or eels on offer, but do

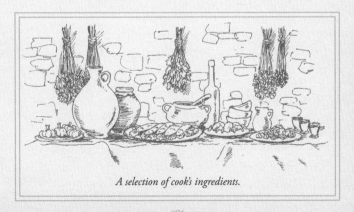

*A selection of cook's ingredients.*

# WATCH WHAT YOU DRINK

Excellent water is provided from the public fountains, brought to Rome by its aqueducts. Visitors are advised not to drink the river water nor to bathe in the Tiber, whatever your customs are at home. Contact with the water from the Tiber will result in illness (even the Germans resident in the city have given up bathing their newborn children in the river), and like the Romans you should use the public fountains. Do not eat fish caught downstream from the city—this is unlikely in any case, since so few survive in the foul water.

not eat anything caught in the Tiber. Like the land-based animals, fish and seafood are served up with spiced and sweetened sauces. There are also innumerable sausages, hams, and cured meats.

## WINE

Wine is usually diluted and is often spiced and sweetened. You may find one or two parts honey mixed with four or five parts wine, a dash of peppercorns, and some strands of saffron. The drink is sickly sweet. The best wines still come from Italy; Falernian originated from the marshes of the coastal plains, but is not the only good wine to be had.

The Romans have introduced wine to many places—although beer is still drunk in the north.

To ensure that you do not smell of wine after over-indulging you can obtain tablets from the perfumier to sweeten the breath.

## PRICES

Expect to pay at most 30 denarii per sextarius for the major Italian wines: Falernian, Sabine, Picene, or Tiburtine. Other aged wines tend to cost a little less (around 16–24 denarii per sextarius), and even less for ordinary unaged wines (8 denarii per sextarius).

You will pay more per pound for pork than beef (12 and 8 denarii at the most, respectively). 10 dormice will cost you 40 denarii, while 10 sparrows will set you back 16 denarii. River fish cost about a third of the price of the best sea fish—you can pay anything from 6 to 24 denarii per pound.

# MONEY, WEIGHTS, AND MEASURES

 ONE OF ROME'S GREAT ACHIEVEMENTS HAS BEEN TO DEVELOP AN INTERNATIONAL CURRENCY, BUT IN RECENT TIMES WE HAVE SEEN A DEVALUATION OF ROMAN COINS, AND INFLATION FUELED BY GREED. SIX YEARS AGO, DIOCLETIAN REFORMED T H E COINAGE AND SET IT ONCE AGAIN ON A FIRMER FOOTING. IT IS HOPED THE PROCESS WILL NOT HAVE TO BE REPEATED, BUT THERE ARE RUMORS OF A FURTHER REFORM. JUST AS THERE IS A STANDARD COINAGE, SO THERE IS ALSO A STANDARD SET OF WEIGHTS AND MEASURES.

Wherever possible, visitors should use newer coins rather than earlier ones of less value. Be careful to check your change. There are constant revisions of the coinage: for example, all Italian sestertii have recently been reduced to the value of a denarius. It can be concluded that there is inflation fueled by greedy sellers.

In state and legal documents you will find prices given in denarii, but you will also encounter the aureus, argenteus, sestertius, as, and nummus. These coins provide a system of exchange, whereby 1 aureus is worth 25 silver coins, 100 sestertii, 200 denarii, 2000 asses, and 20,000 nummi.

Diocletian has addressed the issue of silver and gold content in earlier coinage by insisting that all argentei struck in the mints bear the mark XCVI and contain only silver. The new sestertii are marked with XXI and are made of silvered bronze. Some 60 aurei can be produced from a pound of gold, while 96 argentei can be produced from a pound of silver, but the argenteus seems to have fallen out of circulation, perhaps because its high silver content makes it a valued item in its own right. The denarius is valued at half a sestertius, and there are ten asses to the denarius.

With the expected fixing of maximum prices and wages in the near future, the reformed coinage is part of a package of reforms intended to address the problems of inflation and devaluation of the coinage that have occurred over the last century or more. Many of the earlier coins have been recalled and melted down, and the mint at Alexandria has been closed.

## WEIGHTS

The Roman libra, or pound, is divided into 12 unciae, or ounces, as follows:

uncia = 1
sextans = 2
triens = 3
quadrans = 4
quincunx = 5
semis = 6
septunx = 7
bes = 8
dodrans = 9
dextans = 10
deunx = 11

The uncia has further subdivisions:

sescuncia = $1^1/_2$
semiuncia = $^1/_2$
sicilicus = $^1/_4$
sextula = $^1/_6$
semisextula = $^1/_{12}$
scripulum = $^1/_{24}$

## MEASURES

The basic unit of liquid volume is the sextarius, subdivided as follows (most measures will be found in bars, except the smallest measure, the cochlearum, which is mostly used in medicine):

hemina = $^1/_2$
quartarius = $^1/_4$
acetabulum = $^1/_8$
cyathus = $^1/_{12}$
cochlearum = $^1/_{48}$

Wine is also measured by the congius, equivalent to 6 sextarii or 12 heminae. There are 8 congii to the amphora and 20 amphorae to the culleus.

There are 16 sextarii to the modius—the most common dry measure used, for example, to measure corn or other dry goods.

*The modius is used as the measure of dry goods such as corn.*

# SHOPPING

WHEN GOING TO A CITY WHERE EVERYTHING IS AVAILABLE, YOU WILL BE EXPECTED TO PURCHASE GIFTS FOR YOUR FAMILY AND FRIENDS. YOU MAY ALSO NEED A GIFT OR TWO IF VISITING AT THE SATURNALIA. ALL OF ROME'S STREETS ARE LINED WITH SHOPS AND THERE ARE ALSO SPECIALIZED MARKETS, AUCTIONS, AND MANY SOUVENIRS TO BE HAD.

## MARKETS IN ROME

You will find a number of *macella* in Rome. There is the macellum of Livia on the Esquiline Hill and the Macellum Magnum on the Caelian Hill—the dome was built by Nero and is a worthy sight in its own right. However, you will also find many other markets that are held in far less magnificent settings. There is a schedule of weekly markets with some sellers coming from as far away as the Bay of Neapolis.

Markets can be found in most towns, often held in a purpose-built macellum. Prices are regulated by the cities' magistrates, who also scrutinize weights and measures in order to ensure fair trading.

*One of Rome's bustling indoor markets.*

## AUCTIONS

All sorts of goods are auctioned in the basilicas of Rome: bricks, slaves, antiques, statues, marble, furniture, in fact almost everything. The auctioneer will usually try to demonstrate the value of the goods on sale and to create an atmosphere of fevered expectation. On completion of a deal, a promissory note is made and suitably witnessed, with requirements for delivery and payment stipulated.

## GIFTS AND SOUVENIRS

Gift-giving is very much part of Rome's winter festival, the Saturnalia, so much so that a part of the city is named after the gifts: the Sigillaria. Every type of gift is available here, from gold-plated litters to small ceramic figurines. There is something for everyone, and there is always the option of viewing rather than buying. It also perhaps offers the best chance of buying a memento for yourself or a gift for those at home.

## PRICES

The following guide is given to allow visitors to know if they are being fleeced (the highest acceptable price is given).

Shoes vary according to quality: equestrian shoes are the cheapest at 70 denarii; senators' shoes 150 denarii; whereas patrician shoes come in at 100 denarii. Women's boots will set you back 60 denarii; whereas a good pair of work boots

will cost anything up to 120 denarii. As for luxury materials, white silk will cost 12,000 denarii per pound; if dyed purple, the price may even reach 150,000 denarii per pound. Wool is cheaper, ranging from 50 to 175 denarii if washed, but if dyed purple the cost will be more like 50,000 denarii per pound. Gold costs up to 50,000 denarii per pound, with a labor charge of 5,000 denarii per pound.

## DELIVERY

If you wish to send your purchases any distance in the Roman empire, expect to pay large sums. A donkey load will cost you 4 denarii per mile, and if you fill a 1200-pound wagon you will pay 20 denarii per mile. If you are sending goods by sea, 1 modius will cost you 16 denarii from Rome to Alexandria or vice-versa. The main cost is getting your stuff to Portus safely.

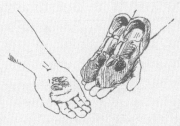

*Prices are liable to change in Rome, so check what you can expect to be charged upon your arrival.*

# POSTAGE AND COMMUNICATIONS

THERE IS NO PUBLIC POSTAL SYSTEM AS SUCH IN THE ROMAN EMPIRE, BUT POST IS TAKEN BY TRAVELERS, AND CERTAIN PERSONS ARE DESIGNATED TO CARRY MESSAGES TO A CERTAIN PLACE (THESE ARE OFTEN SLAVES OR FREEDMEN OF A HOUSEHOLD). THERE ARE ALSO PROFESSIONAL COURIERS WHO WILL TAKE CORRESPONDENCE TO ANOTHER PERSON AT A DESIGNATED PLACE FOR A FEE.

Nearly every section of the Roman bureaucracy has its own set of imperial messengers. The amount of communication involved between the departments and the emperors is enormous.

Governors of provinces are in constant correspondence with the relevant emperor and his court to ensure that they are applying the law correctly and so on.

It is interesting that this is not a new phenomenon. The tenth book of Pliny's *Epistulae* contains correspondence between the governor of Bithynia and the emperor Trajan, and demonstrates that the problems that beset the empire some 200 years ago are similar to those faced today.

### SENDING A LETTER

The system of sending letters is fairly basic, but you need certain information before you begin: where is the person you wish to write to? Unless you know, you cannot get a letter to them. Hence, if a friend is planning a trip to Mediolanum, for example, ask him where he will stop on the way—from this you can estimate where to send a letter in order to reach him at the right time.

On receipt of your letter, he may hand your courier one written recently, or may write a quick reply before your courier returns to you.

When traveling, you may find numerous letters awaiting you at stopping places. Couriers tend to travel rather faster than you will as a visitor, hence they will overtake you, leave the correspondence to await you, and pass you on the road on their way back. To understand the system, examine Cicero's published *Letters to Atticus*, paying careful attention to the dates and places of composition.

# THE CURSUS PUBLICUS

Often mistakenly thought to be a postal service, the Cursus Publicus is a system designed to provide a transport infrastructure for those carrying public information, or for public officials. For example an imperial procurator might use up to 10 wagons or 30 mules, or a combination of mules and wagons. Officials also have the right to requisition the animals and wagons of provincials for public purposes. Most cities and many villages are required to provide ten wagons and as many mules as necessary; they are paid for each wagon or mule used. (The system of payment is currently under review and might be abolished in the future.)

*The cursus publicus is the empire's network for official communications.*

# IF YOU ARE ILL

MOST FORMS OF MEDICINE ARE PRACTICED IN ROME.
VISITORS SHOULD GAIN A RUDIMENTARY KNOWLEDGE OF
THE TREATMENTS AVAILABLE (CELSUS IS WORTH READING
PRIOR TO ARRIVAL IN THE CITY), SO THAT THEY MAY BE
INFORMED OF THE NATURE OF THE CURES SUGGESTED.

Medicine arrived in Rome just over 500 years ago, when the first Greek doctor, Archanthus, set up shop. A wound specialist, Archanthus was quickly renamed the "executioner." However, Asclepiades redeemed the reputation of doctors with his combination of treatments: gentle exercise, food, wine, massages, and baths to dislodge blockages within the body preventing the fluids

*The medical pioneer Asclepiades.*

circulating. Others preferred cold-water plunges for their patients; these are said to have cured the emperor Augustus, but probably finished off his nephew Marcellus.

### MODERN MEDICINE

In more recent times, Galen of Pergamum has produced some astounding medical observations, not least that a woman's pulse rate increases if the name of her lover is mentioned—which is also of utility if you should wish to identify an adulterer. He did much to push forward the understanding of the body by observing criminals after punishment.

There are also female doctors in the city, and numerous midwives. Doctors continue to have a reputation for killing their patients and have been suspected of poisoning them, including the emperor Marcus Aurelius at the instigation of his son Commodus.

WHAT TO EXPECT

# CATO'S CABBAGE CURES

Unlike most medical practices, Cato's recipe to purge an illness is the same for men, women, and children. Every morning, if you have no fever, a very small glass of deep red wine is drunk (for those with a fever, water is substituted). Then comes a broth that tastes of cabbage with a hint of cumin and is rather salty, before you are finally presented with a plate of al dente cabbage.

Cabbage is also used to make a poultice that is placed on wounds, swellings, and boils. Dislocated joints are also often treated with a cabbage poultice as are any number of other ailments.

If you complain of arthritis, you may be prescribed raw cabbage chopped up, mixed with coriander, and pickled cabbage mixed with both vinegar and honey. There is also the "Catonian total purge" made from a powerful concoction composed of ham scraps, beet plants, mussels, some fish, a scorpion, snails, lentils, and various other items. It is mixed with Coan wine. The taste is surprisingly agreeable. Most patients are given three doses—do bear in mind, though, that it is essential to rest but also to be not too distant from a vacant toilet, of which there are 144 public ones in Rome.

Romans tend to believe that doctors swearing the Hippocratic oath are actually swearing to murder all persons who are not Greek—an example of something being lost in translation, perhaps.

The sick traveler seeking a truly Roman experience will be able to find a local who will provide them with the recipes for one of Cato's cabbage cures (details may also be found in Cato's *De Agricultura*).

# CRIME AND THE LAW

THERE IS NO PUBLIC PROSECUTOR IN ROME AND IT IS UP TO PRIVATE INDIVIDUALS TO INITIATE LEGAL PROCEEDINGS IF A CRIME HAS BEEN COMMITTED. THESE *DELATORES* (ACCUSERS) BENEFIT FROM A CUT OF THE PROPERTY CONFISCATED FROM THE GUILTY, HENCE MANY ARE READY TO BRING ACCUSATIONS AGAINST OTHERS. THE LAW FAVORS THE RICH AND THE RESOLUTION OF THEIR DISPUTES, THEREFORE VISITORS MUST ENSURE THAT THEY DO NOT BREAK THE LAW IN ROME.

Rome has developed a complex body of law that addresses most offenses. This is not a coincidence—there is much crime in Rome, and visitors should take care, particularly at night.

The prefect of the *vigiles* (the night watch) is responsible for fire-fighting, but can also warn the careless or issue punishment beatings. He has jurisdiction over burglars, arsonists, thieves, and robbers caught by his soldiers.

Serious crimes are referred to the urban prefect, a very senior senator, who deals with all criminal matters within Rome and up to 100 miles outside. He has the power to deport the rich, condemn the poor to the mines, and even sentence men and women to death.

cohorts openly carry a sword and short knife, and the Praetorian Guard are similarly equipped. The vigiles are seen at night and carry equipment to enable them to pull down buildings and create fire-breaks in the city.

A number of soldiers also carry equipment for the torture of slaves to ensure that they tell the prefect the truth. Over the last century, torture has been employed on many of the poorer citizens in the name of extracting truth and justice. It would seem the Romans assume the rich are more honest than the poor! It is not unknown for soldiers to assault individuals in the city in response to even the most trivial of offenses, so be on your guard.

## POLICING THE CITY

Visitors are sure to see some of the 32,000 soldiers who police the city. The soldiers of the urban

## CRIME AND PUNISHMENT

Punishment can be separated into the *quaestio* (interrogation under torture) and the *supplicium*

# MAJOR CRIMES IN ROME

What is considered reasonable by one society is abhorrent to another, so it pays to be familiar with what is considered criminal behavior in Rome. Major offenses include: abduction, adultery, arson, bigamy, corruption of a slave, forgery, homicide, incest, kidnapping, parricide, rape, sexual assault, theft, and treason.

In the past Rome has tolerated the religions of others, but times are changing. Fifty years ago, the emperor Decius' edict enforced religious conformity, with the exception of the Jews. Christians felt the full force of the edict, and there are rumors that over the next few years Diocletian will enforce this edict again. If this happens then those who will persist in following the Christian religion will lose all juridical privileges and be subject to torture.

*The urban cohorts police the streets of Rome.*

(punishment). The latter acts both as retribution and deterrence, as any visitor will see from the criminals decaying on their crosses along the roads leading into Rome.

Punishments also take place in public, and the Romans have created new and ghastlier penances—the last century has even seen adulterers tied together and set on fire. The legal process is less brutal for the rich, who at the worst suffer a loss of status or exile. Visitors who break laws are sure to feel Rome's full retribution.

# REFERENCES
# AND RESOURCES

*This section contains reference material often
relating to matters that Romans will expect visitors to
know. It is worth spending some time learning the
material here—you need a knowledge of numerals,
knowledge of the rulers of Rome, at least a passing
acquaintance with the literature of this most civilized
of cities, and at least a little Latin to get by with—a
few phrases are suggested here, but really you need to
study the language and learn the grammar that
underpins it. However, nothing can completely prepare
you for Rome, the largest and most cultured city in
the world.*

# RULERS OF ROME

ROMULUS, THE FOUNDER OF ROME, WAS THE FIRST
KING. THERE FOLLOWED 244 YEARS OF MONARCHY, THE
CHRONOLOGY OF WHICH IS DISPUTABLE AT BEST. THIS WAS
FOLLOWED BY 463 YEARS OF REPUBLICAN GOVERNMENT,
ENDED BY THE DICTATORSHIP OF JULIUS CAESAR. CAESAR'S
ADOPTED SON AND GRANDNEPHEW, OCTAVIAN, ESTABLISHED
THE CURRENT MODE OF GOVERNMENT BY EMPERORS, AND HE
WAS INDEED THE FIRST EMPEROR. TODAY, EMPERORS HAVE
RULED ROME FOR SOME 300 YEARS—A SYSTEM THAT SUITS
THE GOVERNMENT OF AN IMMENSE TERRITORY, AN EMPIRE
EXTENDING ACROSS EUROPE, ASIA, AND AFRICA.

### DATES IN YEARS BEFORE PRESENT

| | |
|---|---|
| 1052–1016 | *Rule of Latin and Sabine kings* |
| 949–808 | *Rule of the Etruscan kings* |
| 808–345 | *Rule of the Roman republic* |
| 345–343 | *Julius Caesar —Dictator (start of the Julio-Claudian Dynasty)* |
| 326–286 | *Augustus—first emperor of Rome* |
| 286–263 | *Tiberius* |
| 263–259 | *Caligula* |
| 259–246 | *Claudius I* |
| 246–230 | *Nero* |
| 231 | *Year of the Four emperors: Galba, Otho, Vitellius, and Vespasian (first emperor of the Flavian Dynasty)* |
| 231–221 | *Vespasian* |
| 221–220 | *Titus* |
| 220–204 | *Domitian* |

*Marcus Aurelius*

| | |
|---|---|
| **204–202** | Nerva (first emperor of the Nervan-Antonine Dynasty) |
| **202–183** | Trajan |
| **183–162** | Hadrian |
| **162–139** | Antoninus Pius |
| **139–123** | Marcus Aurelius (ruled jointly with Lucius Verus until 130 years ago) |
| **123–107** | Commodus |
| **106** | Pertinax |
| **106** | Dedius Julianus |
| **106–89** | Septimius Severus (first emperor of the Severan Dynasty) |
| **89–83** | Caracalla (ruled jointly with Geta for one year) |

Octavian, who was awarded the title Augustus by the Senate and ruled Rome as its first emperor around 300 years before the time of writing.

| | | | |
|---|---|---|---|
| **83–82** | Macrinus | **47–41** | Valerian |
| **82–78** | Elagabalus | **40–32** | Gallienus |
| **78–65** | Alexander Severus | **32–30** | Claudius II |
| **65–62** | Maximus Thrax | **30–25** | Aurelian |
| **62** | Gordian I | **25–24** | Tacitus |
| **62** | Gordian II | **24** | Florianus |
| **62** | Balbinus and Pupienus ruled jointly | **24–18** | Probus |
| | | **18–17** | Carus |
| **62–56** | Gordian III | **17–15** | Carinus (jointly with Numerian for one year) |
| **56–51** | Philip the Arabian | | |
| **51–49** | Decius | **16–present** | Diocletian (ruled jointly with Maximian from 14 years ago) |
| **49** | Hostilianus | | |
| **49–47** | Trebonianus Gallus | | |
| **47** | Aemilianus | | |

# LANGUAGE, LITERATURE, AND RECOMMENDED READING

THERE ARE SO MANY EXCELLENT ROMAN WRITERS THAT IT IS DIFFICULT TO DO JUSTICE TO THEM ALL. HERE ARE SELECTED ONLY A FEW OF THE CLASSICS, THOSE THAT ARE MOST LIKELY TO ENDURE THE TEST OF TIME.

## CICERO

A classic author and orator, Cicero's speeches persuaded crowds of thousands to change their minds time and again. *De Domo Sua* (*on his house*) reveals the struggles between him and Clodius, and all the brutality of an unstable system of government. In contrast, his philosophical works offer advice on how to act (*De Officiis*), on the nature of the republic (*De Re Publica*), and on the nature of the law (*De Legibus*). Other works provide an augur's insight into the nature of the pagan gods of Rome. His posthumously published letters reveal a quite different use of the Latin language from his other works: the correspondence with Atticus contains gossip, interjections, and information on his family.

*M. Tullius Cicero*

## HISTORIES OF ROME

There are numerous diachronic or annalistic histories of Rome from its birth through to the time of writing. Dio Cassius composed his *History of Rome* under the Severans in Greek, offering a real understanding of power under Rome's rulers. Earlier classics include Tacitus' *Histories* and *Annales* and also Livy's *Ab Urbe Condita* (*from the foundation of the city*).

*Pliny the Elder*

provides an understanding of the more ancient buildings of Rome constructed or rebuilt under Augustus. Meanwhile Celsus' *De Medicina* provides a handy guide to the practice of medicine, but is now rather dated—it should be consulted alongside the works of the Greek doctor Galen. And an understanding of agricultural practice can be gained from Columella's work.

For those interested in the natural world then Pliny the Elder's *Historia Naturalis* is a must, as it covers nearly every natural phenomenon to be found in the Roman Empire in the course of its pages.

### BIOGRAPHY

Suetonius' biographies of the first emperors are the standard works that provide a full discussion of character—a trend followed by more recent writers of biography. Plutarch also provides biographies of figures from the republic, in Greek.

### TECHNICAL ARTS

If you are looking for insights into Rome's technical mastery of the world then there are many suitable volumes. Among them Vitruvius' *De Architectura* written under Augustus remains the classic treatise on the subject and

*Plutarch*

There is a great deal to recommend the many histories of Rome, biographies of its great rulers, and descriptions of the nature, practices, and customs you will find there. However, if you want to see into the heart of the Romans themselves then the visitor should perhaps look to Rome's speeches, novels, and poetry.

### RHETORIC AND PUBLIC SPEAKING

Quintilian's extensive writing on this subject is the major point of reference, but do consult actual speeches as well. Pliny the Younger's *Panegyricus*—a speech in praise of Trajan (delivered in front of him over the course of many hours) is an ingenious piece of flattery.

### NOVELS

The Roman novel is an impressive genre, perhaps only bettered by those novels written in Greek.

Among the best is Petronius' classic novel *Satyricon*. It tells of the travails of its narrator, Encolpius, and his lover, the handsome pubescent boy Giton—and in doing so provides an enthralling insight into life in the city of Rome.

### POETRY

There is a great wealth of much-loved poetry from the Augustan age. Among the great poets are Quintus Horatius Flaccus (Horace) who is best known for his *Odes* and *Epodes*, both collections of poems, while P. Vergilius Maro (Virgil) is celebrated for his epic poem, the *Aeneid*.

This engrossing narrative tells the tale of Aeneas, who fled the downfall of Troy and traveled to Italy. It was here, as had been prophesied, that he was to become the ancestor of the Romans. However, as was also the case for his Greek counterpart Ulysses, his journey from Troy was far from straightforward, and the first half of the *Aeneid* deals with his tortuous wanderings. Perhaps the

*G. Plinius Caecilius Secundus, known as Pliny the Younger.*

most notable event of these is the occasion upon which Aeneas falls in love with Dido, the queen of Carthage. Torn between his heart and the duty to fulfill his destiny Aeneas reluctantly departs for Italy; however, in her grief Dido commits suicide, and dooms Aeneas' heirs to war with her people—a destiny that was fulfilled in the series of Punic Wars between 563 and 445 years before the time of writing.

Once he had landed in Italy Aeneas waged war against the Latins, and the poem concludes with him killing Turnus, the king of the Rutuli, in single combat.

Virgil died before he could finish the *Aeneid*, so the story of his marriage to Lavinia, and the birth of their son Silvius remains untold. In spite of the excellence of the *Aeneid* it is not all that Virgil is known for, and his other acclaimed works include his pastoral endeavors: the *Georgics* and the *Eclogues*.

In counterpoint to these authors is the Roman genre of love poetry—Publius Ovidius Naso's (Ovid's) work remains classic. His *Metamorphoses* is his most celebrated work, and it tells the story of both the creation of the world and its history.

Alongside this earlier works such as the comprehensive poems of Gaius Valerius Catullus are well worth reading.

*P. Vergilius Maro (Virgil) the author of the* Aeneid.

Indeed, such epigrams are particularly useful for conjuring up the nature of Rome's streets as seen by the elite of Rome. Marcus Valerius Martialis (Martial) provides 14 books of these brief, pithy poems.

Also worth investigation is the metropolitan genre of satire: Decimus Iunius Iuvenalis (Juvenal), Aulus Persius Flaccus (Persius), and Horace all have witty takes on the city and indeed the viewer's or reader's expectations of the city.

# THE ROMAN ALPHABET
# AND NUMERALS

THE LATIN ALPHABET IS RELATIVELY EASY TO FOLLOW, AND CHILDREN ARE TAUGHT TO RECITE ITS LETTERS FIRST FORWARD FROM A–Z AND THEN BACKWARD FROM Z–A, BEFORE FINALLY COMBINING THE TWO FROM AZ, BY, CX ALL THE WAY TO ZA. THIS IS PERHAPS THE BEST WAY FOR A TRAVELER TO LEARN IT BEFORE ARRIVING IN ROME. THERE ARE 23 LETTERS IN TOTAL: ABCDEFGHIKLMNOPQRSTVXYZ.

It must be said that the Latin alphabet is a remarkable device, yet it perhaps seems a little strange that the Romans did not simply adopt the existing Greek alphabet from the cities of southern Italy. But no, we have a fusion of two sets of script: the Greek, and the Etruscan letter forms that are related to the Punic language. Hence, the letters B, E, H, I, K, M, N, O, T, X, Y, Z have much in common with their Greek equivalents, while the other letters show greater congruence with Etruscan letter forms. The character Z is a relatively recent addition; although in the Greek alphabet it is the seventh letter, in the Roman it is the twenty-third to reflect its novelty.

## ROMAN LETTERING

Inscriptions can quite easily be found on most public buildings recording the dedication of the building, who paid for it, and even how much it cost to build. The curious visitor may find much of interest.

A major innovation in Roman letter form is that the strokes of the letters are not of the same weight, some are thick, whereas others are thin.

When carved onto stone, the letter forms are easily discerned—but note that the mason has used thin and thick chisels according to the element of the letter in question.

Some of the larger inscriptions have been filled with bronze so that the lettering might, when clean, reflect the sun's rays and further enhance the effect of the inscription. It should be stated that the letter forms are far more beautiful than any others in the world today, and that they are likely to stand the test of time.

# ROMAN NUMERALS

Roman numbers are fairly simple to use, at least until the number increases to a size where the potential for differing representations means that mistakes can easily occur.

| | |
|---|---|
| I = 1 | XX = 20 |
| II = 2 | XXX = 30 |
| III = 3 | XL or XXXX = 40 |
| IV or IIII = 4 | L = 50 |
| V = 5 | LX = 60 |
| VI = 6 | LXX = 70 |
| VII = 7 | LXXX = 80 |
| VIII = 8 | XC or LXXXX = 90 |
| IX or VIIII = 9 | C = 100 |
| X = 10 | CC = 200 |
| XI = 11 | CCC = 300 |
| XII = 12 | CD or CCCC = 400 |
| XIII = 13 | D = 500 |
| XIV or XIIII = 14 | DC = 600 |
| XV = 15 | DCC = 700 |
| XVI = 16 | DCCC = 800 |
| XVII = 17 | CM or DCCCC = 900 |
| XVIII = 18 | M = 1000 |
| XIX or XVIIII = 19 | |

# USEFUL TERMS AND PHRASES

MANY COME TO ROME WITH THE EXPECTATION OF A UNIFIED
STANDARD LATIN SPELLING AND GRAMMAR. SUCH IDEALISTS
ARE FREQUENTLY DISAPPOINTED, OR SPEND THEIR TIME
CONCENTRATING ON THE MINUTIAE OF THE LANGUAGE AND
THE IDEA THAT IT SHOULD BE SPOKEN IN A CERTAIN WAY.
THESE PEOPLE ARE NIT-PICKERS, BUT THERE ARE LOTS OF
THEM—MOSTLY ACADEMICS WITH LITTLE IMAGINATION.

Just as spelling is quite varied, so is pronunciation; even the emperor Vespasian was subjected to criticism for his rather rustic forms of Latin words. There is a great difference between written literary Latin and the spoken word. The language found in the 500-year-old plays of Plautus and Terence reflects an idiom associated with polite society of the time. However, few people speak Latin in this form today.

## SOME USEFUL PHRASES

**Salve!** *Hello*

**Vale!** *Goodbye*

**Qui vales?** *How are you?*

**Haud male.** *Not bad.*

**Salve. Te vonvienisse volup est** *Hello. Pleased to meet you.*

**Quid nomen tibi est?** *What is your name?*

**Unde es?** *Where are you from?*

**Quot annos nata/us es tu?** *How old are you?*

**Esne tu paterfamilias?** *Are you a head of a family?*

**Die dulci fruere.** *Have a nice day.*

**Gratias multa** *Thanks a lot.*

**Cave canem.** *Beware of the dog.*

**Ubi est forum?** *Where is the forum?*

**Ubi est amphiteatrum, quaeso?** *Where is the amphitheater please?*

**Estne balnea in ea vicinia?** *Is there a bath-house nearby?*

**Satine caloris tibi est?** *Hot enough for you?*

**Turbane magna vehiculorum obviam erat tibi venienti huc?** *Was there much traffic on the way over?*

**Quantum Roma abest Cuma?** *How far is it from Rome to Cuma?*

**Da mihi poculum vini.** *I'll have a glass of wine.*

**Quid est illud in vinum?** *What's that in the wine?*

**Cogito sumere potum alterum.** *I think I'll have another drink.*

**Caupo! Etiamnunc!** *Innkeeper! The same again!*

**Re vera, potas bene.** *You really are drinking a lot.*

**Nescio quid dicas.** *I don't know what you are talking about.*

**Quid fit?** *What's happening?*

**Me male habeo.** *I don't feel so good.*

**Quid tibi est?** *What's wrong with you?*

**Fauces dolet, stomachus dolet, caput dolet.** *Throat hurts, stomach hurts, head hurts.*

**Vero?** *Really?*

**Est mihi nullus nummus superfluus.** *I do not have any spare change.*

**Non rape me si placet.** *Please don't rob me.*

**Volo pactum facere.** *I'd like to make a deal.*

**Tempus meum tero.** *I'm wasting my time.*

**Carpe diem.** *Seize the day.*

**Ita erat quando hic adveni.** *It was like that when I got here.*

**Nemo hic adest illius nominis.** *There is no one here by that name.*

**Annus horribilis.** *Ghastly year.*

## COMMON ABBREVIATIONS

| | | | | | | |
|---|---|---|---|---|---|---|
| **AED** | aedilis | aedile | **D N** | dominus noster | our lord/ emperor |
| **ANN** | annos/is | year(s) | **D S** | de suo | from his own money |
| **ANN** | annona | corn supply | **EQ** | eques | Roman knight |
| **AVG** | Augustus | Augustus | | | |
| **CA** | curam agens | taking care | **EXSC** | ex senatus consultum | by decree of the senate |
| **CAP** | capitalis | magistrate overseeing executions | **F** | fecit/ faciundum | did/ to be done |
| | | | **F** | filius/filia | son/ daughter |
| **C V** | clarissimus vir | distinguished man | **H** | heres | heir |
| **COH** | cohors | cohort | **H S E** | hic sita /situs est | s/he lies here |
| **COS** | consul | consul | **IMP** | imperator | emperor |
| **C R** | cives Romani | Roman citizen | | | |
| **CVR** | curavit | took care of | **I O M** | Iupiter Optimus Maximus | Jupiter Best and Greatest |
| **DEC** | decreto | by decree | **L** | libertus | freed slave |
| **DED** | dedit | gave | **LEG** | legio | legion |
| **D M** | Dis Manibus | to the spirits of the dead | **LOC** | locus | place |
| | | | **MIL** | miles | soldier |

| | | | | | |
|---|---|---|---|---|---|
| **NAT** | *natus* | born | **R P** | *res publica* | the state |
| **NOB CAES** | | | **S C** | *senatus consulto* | by decree of the senate |
| | *nobilissimus caesar* | most noble caesar | | | |
| **O H S S** | *ossa hic sita est* | the bones lie here | **S P** | *sua pecunia* | with his own money |
| **OPT** | *optio* | centurion's deputy | **S P Q R** | | |
| | | | | *Senatus Populusque Romanus* | The Senate and the People of Rome |
| **PAR** | *parentes* | parents | | | |
| **P P** | *pater patriae* | father of the country | **TEST** | *testamentum* | will |
| **P M** | *pontifex maximus* | supreme priest | **TR MIL** | | |
| | | | | *tribunus militum* | military tribune |
| **POS** | *posuit* | set this up | **TR PL** | *tribunus plebes* | tribune of the people |
| **P P** | *primus pilus* | chief centurion | | | |
| | | | **V** | *vir* | man |
| **PRAEF** | *praefectus* | prefect | **V** | *vixit* | lived |
| **PRAET** | *praetor* | praetor | **V** | *vivus* | alive |
| **PROCONS** | | | **V** | *vovit* | vowed |
| | *proconsul* | proconsul | | | |
| **PROC** | *procurator* | procurator | **VET** | *veteranus* | veteran |
| **PROV** | *provincia* | province | **VEX** | *vexillatio* | detachment |
| **REST** | *restituit* | restored | **VRB** | *urbana* | urban |

---

# NOTES FOR THE MODERN READER

---

THE MODERN READER NEEDS TO KNOW THAT THE GUIDE WAS WRITTEN FOR VISITORS TO THE CITY IN AD 300. MOST INFORMATION IS CONTEMPORARY, BUT AS WITH ALL THINGS ANCIENT THERE IS AN ELEMENT OF RE-USE OF EARLIER WORKS AND DELIBERATE ARCHAISING OF THE TEXT IN PLACES. THE PRESENT TENSE IS USED THROUGHOUT AND WHERE THE PAST TENSE IS USED IT IS TO SIGNIFY EVENTS EARLIER THAN AD 300.

So, what happened to the empire after AD 300? In AD 301, an edict on maximum wages and prices was introduced. A full scale persecution of the Christians commenced in AD 303. After visiting Rome in that year, two years later Diocletian stepped down, as did Maximian.

They were succeeded by their caesars: Galerius and Constantius. The latter died in AD 306, providing an opportunity for Maximian's son to seize the throne—he was opposed by all including his own father, yet managed to establish his position as emperor. In AD 312, he was defeated in battle by Constantius' son, the emperor Constantine.

## CONSTANTINE AND CHRISTIANITY

Remarkably, Constantine converted to Christianity. He also founded Constantinople as a "New Rome" to rule the eastern half of the empire with its own senate, and administrative offices that matched those found in Rome.

This really was a new age for the Roman Empire, in which cities were renewed, churches were established, and barbarians continued to be fought.

The empire although outwardly Christian still paid heed to the ancestral gods. The emperor Julian (reign: AD 351–4), though brought up a Christian, developed a strong dislike for Christianity since it denied the gods of Roman paganism. The temples of the pagan religion were re-opened, restored, and new ones built—Christianity had not managed to obliterate Rome's ancestral past.

Afterwards, polytheism was to be tolerated by Christian monotheists—even if Christians were only too willing to persecute the pagans, the Jews, and Christian heretics. Even a hundred years after Constantine it would be difficult to substantiate a claim that the empire was a Christian one. Yet, what we see built in the cities of the empire are churches in this period—a new phenomenon.

## ROME DIVIDED

A hundred years on from Diocletian, we find the empire divided between the west ruled from Rome and the east ruled from Constantinople. In both parts of the empire, the army became increasingly populated by barbarians and commanded by their leaders; who struggled to defeat the increasing numbers of invaders from beyond the frontiers—Rome was sacked by the Vandals in AD 455.

Eventually Romulus Augustulus was dethroned by Theodoric in AD 476, who would rule in conjunction with Roman senators and even restore the "Queen of Roads"—the Via Appia.

## MODERN ROME

More than 1,700 years on from the time for which this book was composed, visitors are still able to see the ruins of nearly all the buildings mentioned in the guide. For example, the contemporary project to build the Baths of Diocletian is just a short walk from the railway station, from where visitors can catch the No. 64 bus to the Forum.

Today, you will find numerous statues of the emperors in Rome's many museums—check the Internet for opening times, but also phone ahead for the accuracy of the information.

The following list provides you with some further reading on a number of the topics that are covered in this book.

## HISTORY AND CULTURE

*The Cambridge Ancient History* in 19 volumes provides a full history of the ancient world.

**S. Hornblower and A. Spawforth,** *Oxford Classical Dictionary.*

**G. Shipley, J. Vanderspoel, D. Mattingly, & L. Foxhall,** *The Cambridge Dictionary of Classical Civilisation.*

**S. Mitchell,** *A History of the Later Roman Empire, AD 284–641.*

## ROME

**A. Claridge,** *Rome: An Oxford Archaeological Guide* provides information on most monuments.

**L. Richardson,** *A New Topographical Dictionary of Ancient Rome* gives descriptions of most locations.

**M. Steinby,** *Lexicon Topographicum Urbis Romae* is the definitive multilingual encyclopedia of monuments and places in the city.

**J. Coulston and H. Dodge,**
*Ancient Rome: The Archaeology of the Eternal City* contains articles on most aspects.

### BAY OF NAPLES

**J. H. D'Arms,** *Romans on the Bay of Naples.*

**A. Butterworth and R. Laurence,** *Pompeii: The Living City.*

**R. Laurence,** *Roman Pompeii: Space and Society.*

**R. Harris,** *Pompeii* (a novel).

### TRAVEL

**C. Adams and R. Laurence,** *Travel and Geography in the Roman Empire.*

**L. Casson,** *Travel in the Ancient World.*

**R. Laurence,** *The Roads of Roman Italy: Mobility and Cultural Change.*

### CUSTOMS, HABITS AND ENTERTAINMENT

**J. P. Toner,** *Leisure and Ancient Rome.*

**J. P. V. D. Balsdon,** *Life and Leisure in Ancient Rome.*

**M. Harlow and R. Laurence,** *Growing Up and Growing Old in Ancient Rome.*

### LEGAL MATTERS

**B. W. Frier,** *Landlords and Tenants in Imperial Rome.*

### FOOD AND DRINK

**A. Dalby,** *Food in the Ancient World from A–Z.*

**A. Dalby and S. Grainger,** *The Classical Cookbook.*

**S.J. Fleming,** *Vinum: The Story of Roman Wine.*

### ANCIENT MAP OF ROME

The Severan marble plan that was engraved on marble and clamped to a wall of the temple of Peace can be viewed at: http://formaurbis.stanford.edu

It survives only in fragments, but provides an extremely useful sense of the streets and the monuments of Rome.

### LATIN PHRASES AND LANGUAGE

**H. Beard,** *Latin for All Occasions* contains some of the most useful phrases and translations of what you might really want to say in ancient Rome, if time travel were possible. There are also a number of online lists, for example: www.yuni.com/library/Latin _2.html#F

Finland has its own Latin Radio Station (www.yleradio1.fi/nuntii) on which you can hear Latin at first hand alongside 75,000 other listeners to the news in Latin.

There is also a weather forecast in Latin available at: http://latin.wunderground.com

Elsewhere you may hear the pros recite sections of poetry online at www.fas.harvard.edu/~classics/poetry_and_prose/poetry.html

**ROMAN MEASUREMENTS**

The measurements used throughout this book are Roman, although these are broadly equal modern Imperial measurements. A Roman foot measures 296 mm, roughly equivalent to a modern English foot; 5 feet equals a Roman pace; 125 paces equals a stadium; and 1,000 paces equals a mile (95 yards short of an English mile).

## ROMAN HOURS

Romans divide the 24-hour day into two equal parts, night and day, each of which has 12 hours. The length of the hours varies according to the time of year, with maximum variation from midsummer to midwinter. Sundials are placed at convenient points for reference. The table below converts Roman daylight hours into the modern 24-hour clock. Points further north or south of Rome will vary from this pattern according to latitude.

| Hour | Midsummer | Midwinter |
|------|-----------|-----------|
| 1 | 4:27–5:42 | 7:33–8:17 |
| 2 | 5:42–6:58 | 8:17–9:02 |
| 3 | 6:58–8:13 | 9:02–9:46 |
| 4 | 8:13–9:29 | 9:46–10:31 |
| 5 | 9:29–10:44 | 10:31–11:15 |
| 6 | 10:44–12:00 | 11:15–12:00 |
| 7 | 12:00–13:15 | 12:00–12:44 |
| 8 | 13:15–14:31 | 12:44–13:29 |
| 9 | 14:31–15:46 | 13:29–14:13 |
| 10 | 15:46–17:02 | 14:13–14:58 |
| 11 | 17:02–18:17 | 14:58–15:42 |
| 12 | 18:17–19:33 | 15:42–16:27 |

# INDEX

# INDEX